D0110381

ALSO BY MARTHA BARNETTE

A Garden of Words
The Bill Schroeder Story

The author eating her words.

MARTHA BARNETTE

Ladyfingers and Nun's Tummies

Martha Barnette is co-host, along with Richard Lederer, of the popular public-radio show "A Way with Words," from San Diego's KPBS-FM.

A former reporter for *The* Washington *Post* and editorial writer for the Louisville *Courier-Journal,* she now supports her etymological habit by freelancing for numerous publications, from *The New York Times* to *Salon.* She holds an undergraduate degree in English from Vassar College, and did graduate work in classical languages at the University of Kentucky. Visit her on the web at www.funwords.com.

Ladyfingers & Nun's Tummies

A LIGHTHEARTED LOOK
AT HOW FOODS
GOT THEIR NAMES

Martha Barnette

ASJA Press
New York   Lincoln   Shanghai

Ladyfingers & Nun's Tummies
A Lighthearted Look at How Foods Got Their Names

ASJA Press
an imprint of iUniverse, Inc.

iUniverse books may be ordered through booksellers or
by contacting:

iUniverse
2021 Pine Lake Road, Suite 100
Lincoln, NE 68512
www.iuniverse.com
1-800-Authors (1-800-288-4677)

Author photograph © Gil Courson, LightSpeed Photos, Inc.

ISBN: 0-595-34503-4

Printed in the United States of America

CONTENTS

INTRODUCTION

A Feast of Words

Sometimes the very name of a food tickles our taste buds before a bite of it ever reaches our mouths. *Saltimbocca, tiramisù, teriyaki, shabu-shabu, passion fruit, angel hair, soubise, bubble and squeak, chimichanga, couscous* — rolling any of these words around on our tongues is a sensory experience all its own. Even more delicious are the stories and images behind the names of these and many other foods: The worms in a plateful of *vermicelli,* the ancient goddess inside a bowl of *cereal,* the linguistic mistakes that gave us *peas* and *cherries,* the unrequited passion in an *apple Charlotte,* the altercation that led to *lobster Newburg,* and the naughty joke inside every loaf of *pumpernickel.*

This book reveals the unforgettable pictures and surprising tales tucked into the words we put into our mouths every day. It's also a celebration of our intimate, affectionate relationship with food and drink, and how we use words to describe and understand those connections. Moreover, this book is an exploration of the nature of language itself, of the uniquely human activity of creating, bending, adapting, and adopting new words—and how those words in turn help shape the way we think about the world.

As with my previous book, *A Garden of Words* (Times Books, 1992), this volume is based on my twelve years of study with the irrepressible professor of classical languages, Dr. Leonard Latkovski, who died in 1991. Together we read *Oedipus Rex* in the original, a reading that lasted seven years, because nearly every word in the Greek text set the professor off on fascinating tangents and mesmerizing riffs about the connections between languages as different as English, Italian, Russian, and Sanskrit, which share a prehistoric common ancestor. *A Garden of Words* re-created some of those spirited, far-ranging tutorials, using the names of various flowers as a starting point for etymological romps across the boundaries of time, space, culture, and language.

This book does much the same thing, except that this time the subject is food and drink. Consider it a feast of words, a deipnosophist's delight, a linguistic banquet offered up in the hope of being as entertaining as it is enlightening. Feel free to dig in anywhere, because the chapters can be read in any order.

Chapter 1 discusses foods named for the things they look like, be they animals, clothes, miscellaneous objects, or parts of our own bodies. Chapter 2 explores the considerable role that religious belief has played in the names of many foods and beverages. Chapter 3 reveals food names that arose by mistake, through misunderstandings, mistranslations, and other linguistic mix-ups. This chapter also takes a look at the origins of several English expressions that seem to be food-related but in fact are not—a group that includes such terms as *apple-pie order, big cheese,* and *chowderhead.* Chapter 4 discusses edible eponyms and tasty toponyms, the people and places that bequeathed their names to various foods. In this chapter, we'll also take a brief look at a few instances in which the process worked the other way around and a person was named after a food. Chapter 5 is about foods that are named either for what they do or for what's done to them. Finally, Chapter 6 celebrates a host of English terms that contain hidden images of food and drink, from *alma mater* to *zydeco.*

Think of this as a browsing book—bearing in mind, of course, that *browse* is itself a food-related word, one that originally referred to the action of animals moseying about, leisurely nibbling at whatever buds and leaves look particularly inviting. Only later did *browse* acquire its more modern sense, which includes the action of leisurely wandering through the pages of a book and savoring whatever happens to tickle your mind.

So browse away, and *bon appétit*!

For Deb, of course

1

FROM A
HEAD OF CABBAGE TO
FILET OF SOLE

Foods Named for What They Look Like

When people encounter something new and need to figure out what to call it, they often resort to naming it after something they already know. Consider the porpoise. Long ago, when sailors first happened upon this unfamiliar sea creature, they created a name for it based on its likeness to two other animals, the pig and the fish. The word *porpoise* derives from a combination of the Latin word *porcus,* or "pig" (a linguistic relative of the English *pork,* as well as *porcupine,* from the Latin for "spiny pig"), and *piscis,* or "fish" (a relative of the astrological sign *Pisces* and *pisciform,* or "fish-shaped," as well as those frequent fish entrées on French and Italian menus, *poisson* and *pesce*).

Quite a few food names came about the same way, stemming from the names of foods that were already familiar. The *eggplant,* for example, was so named because the delicate white varieties of this vegetable resemble eggs. Similarly, when tomatoes were first imported into England, they were called *love apples,* because they resembled the more familiar fruit and were also considered aphrodisiacs. (Indeed, this name is a direct translation of the French synonym for "tomato," *pomme d'amour,* and its German counterpart, *Liebesapfel.*) Only later was *love apple* replaced with a form of the indigenous Mexican name, *tomatl.* The same sort of thing happened when the French needed a word for a new root vegetable imported from South America. Although the English decided to call it a *potato,* a name adapted from that of a similar tuber, the French christened it with the much more French-sounding *pomme de terre*—literally, "apple of the earth."

In this chapter, we'll consider some foods named for what they look like, including foods named for everything from worms and rats to dogs and cats. We'll also look at some inanimate objects that have bequeathed their names to various forms of cuisine, from clothing

4

and plants to boats and musical instruments. But first, we'll examine the names of many foods that arose because they resemble our own bodies in various ways. Take, for example, the word *ginseng*. The forked root of the plant that goes by this name looks uncannily like a pair of human legs. This image inspired its name in Mandarin Chinese, *rén shēn*, which means "man root." English speakers later altered *rén shēn* into the more manageable name *ginseng*.

In fact, just about every part of the human body has inspired the name of at least one food. Here we'll explore some of them, starting with a head of cabbage and moving down to filet of sole.

Foods That Look Like Parts of the Body

In his curmudgeonly volume *The Devil's Dictionary*, the nineteenth-century American writer Ambrose Bierce defined the word *cabbage* as "A familiar kitchen-garden vegetable about as large and wise as a man's head." Etymologically speaking, Bierce also had the right idea: the phrase *a head of cabbage* is somewhat redundant, *cabbage* having arisen from an Old North French word for "head," *caboche*, which in turn may be linked to the Latin word for "head," *caput*, making *cabbage* a distant relative of such heady terms as *decapitate*, which was once a common form of *capital punishment*. All these "head" words also share a common ancestor with the term for the "head" of a group, *chief*, as well as

5

kerchief (from the Old French *couvrechef*, "to cover the head"). They're also kin to *achieve* (from the Old French *achever*, literally, "to come to a head"), and *mischief* (from the Old French *meschever*, literally, "to come to a head badly"). Unfortunately, our language has lost the use of the perfectly good word *bonchief* as a synonym for "good fortune, prosperity, easy circumstances"—something, in other words, that "comes to a head in a good way." For some reason, this handy word dropped out of English usage during the late sixteenth century.[1]

Another "head" food is the hard, salty Greek cheese *kefalotyri*, which is often pressed into molds that resemble skulls or hats. Literally, its Greek name means "head cheese." The *kefalo-* in *kefalotyri* is a relative of other English words pertaining to the head, such as the medical term for an inflammation of what's inside it, *encephalitis*, and *cephalopod*, the term for those marine creatures such as octopus and squid, which seem to be, as their scientific name literally suggests, mostly "heads and feet." The *-tyri*, or "cheese," in *kefalotyri* is related

---

[1] The French word for "cabbage," *choux*, doubles as the name for a small, flaky pastry originally shaped into little balls that apparently put someone in mind of cabbages. Unlike the English word *cabbage*, however, the French *choux* is a product of the Latin word *caulis*, meaning "stem." This makes the French *choux* a linguistic relative of various other "stemmed" and "cabbagelike" foods, including *cauliflower*, *kohlrabi*, and *kale*. All these words are also the etymological kin of the Dutch word for "cabbage," *kool*, which in turn led to the English word for a cabbage-based salad, *coleslaw*.

to the *-ter* in the English word *butter,* a word that arose from a combination of the Greek *bous,* or "cow," and *turos,* "cheese."

A headful of hair inspired words for foods that are similarly stringy, such as *capelli d'angelo,* or *angel-hair pasta.* In Germany, meanwhile, a dish of fish filets that curl up tightly when smoked is called *Schillerlocken,* commemorating the spectacularly curly locks of that country's beloved eighteenth-century poet Johann Christoph Friedrich von Schiller. (In contrast, "Bald Goethe" cookies, or, in German, *Goetheglatzen,* are flat and sugar-coated on one side and rounded on the top, honoring the bald and beloved author Johann Wolfgang von Goethe.)

From the Malay word for "hair," *rambut,* comes the name of the succulent red fruit covered with soft spines, the *rambutan.* In the Gujarati language of India, cotton candy goes by the name *buddhi na vaal,* or "old woman's hair," while the same wispy sweet is likened to facial hair in France, where it's called *barbe à papa,* or "Dad's beard."

Two supper-table favorites in the southern United States have eyes in their names: *black-eyed peas,* which look as though they have one, and *red-eye gravy,* a mixture of ham drippings and coffee, so called because its heavier ingredients settle into a dark red "eye" at the bottom of the bowl. In France, incidentally, each of those little round oil spots floating on top of a bowl of gravy is called an *œil,* or "eye," and a particularly weak gravy, which has few of them, is said to be *aveugle,* or "blind." Eyes also peek out from the dark centers of Austrian cookies known as *Schwarzäuglein,* or "black eyes." And in Romania, fried eggs are called *oua ochiuri,* literally, "eggs that look like eyes"—which, come to think of it, they do.

Another "face" food is the spicy, edible flower known as the *nasturtium,* which has a "nose" in its name. Often tossed into salads for added color and zest, the nasturtium's bright yellow and orange blossoms take their name from the Latin words for "nose-twister" because of their pungent, nose-twisting flavor. *Nasturtium* shares a common linguistic root with such words as *nasal* and *nose.* The latter part of its name is related to such twisted and twisting words as *contortion, tortuous,* and that "wringing out" of another person, *extortion.*

Our mouths have inspired several terms for the foods that go into them. The *bouchée,* that puff pastry usually filled with creamed seafood, has a name that literally translates from the French as "mouthful." From the same source comes the Albanian word for "bread," *bukë,* as well as the obsolete English word *bouche,* which *Webster's Third New International Dictionary* defines as "an allowance of food and drink for a retinue in a royal or noble household." (These "mouth" words are also related to the Italian *bocca,* or "mouth," which appears in the picturesque food word *saltimbocca.* This dish of spiced, stuffed meat has a name that literally means "it leaps into the mouth.") Luscious lips, meanwhile, are celebrated by the Turkish pastry that resembles them, *∂ilber ∂u∂agi,* "lips of the darling" or "lovely woman's lips."

Inside our mouths lies the inspiration for *linguine,* an Italian word that means "little tongues." *Linguine* shares a linguistic root with several other tongue-related words, including *language, linguist, lingo, bilingual,* and *linguipotence,* the last of these being a majestic-sounding word (accented on the second syllable) that means "mastery of languages." Many lexicographers surmise that *lolly,* a dialectal term for "tongue" in northern England, inspired the word for the candy that makes a distinctive sound when yanked from a sucking mouth, *lollipop.*

"Ears" stick out of food words in several languages. The round, convex pasta known in Italian as *orecchietti* has a name that means "little ears." In Poland, the term for "little ears" is *uszka,* which also denotes a type of egg-dough ravioli that is stuffed with mushrooms and added to soups. (Incidentally, a close etymological relative of the Polish *uszka* is the Russian *ushi,* or "ears," a word that figures prominently in a colorful food phrase, *Ne veshai lapshu na ushi.* Roughly translated, this means "Don't try to put one over on me"—but literally, it's "Don't hang noodles from my ears.") These "ear" words are also the linguistic relatives of the German *Ohr,* or "ear," which appears in the name of the long, oval, deep-fried cookies called *Hasenöhrl,* or "rabbit ear," as well as the German cakes called *Schweinöhren,* or "pig's ears." Then there's that staple of carnival midway fare, the flat, oversized pastries sprinkled with powdered sugar that are known in this country as *elephant ears.*

All these words—*orecchietti, uszka, ushi,* and *ears*—come from a prehistoric root meaning "ear," which also gave us the English *aural* and *ormer,* a shortening of the French *oreille-de-mer,* or "ear of the sea," an ear-shaped abalone. The same root produced the Latin *auricula,* or "little ear," which is part of the scientific name *Auricularia auriculajudae,* which is applied to an ear-shaped fungus popular among Asian cooks. In China, this fungus goes by a name that translates as *cloud ear,* and in English this rounded, delicately flavored growth goes by a direct translation of its Chinese name. (In Thailand, however, the same fungus is called a *het kanoo,* or "rat's ear.") Sometimes, as the latter half of its Latin name suggests, *cloud ear* also goes by the name *Judas ear.* The reason: this fungus usually grows on elder trees, the type from which Judas Iscariot supposedly hanged himself after betraying Jesus.

Ozen Haman, or "Haman's ear," is a cookie popular in Israel. It is baked to commemorate the story of Haman, an official of the Persian Empire who plotted to kill all the Jews under his domain. However, thanks to the efforts of Israelite heroes Esther and Mordecai, Haman's plot was foiled at the eleventh hour, a victory now celebrated on the Jewish holiday of Purim. A three-cornered version of this cookie, traditionally featuring dough wrapped around a sweet mixture of poppy seeds, prunes, or apricots, is popular in the United States, where it's known as *Haman tashen,* or *hamantaschen,* literally, "Haman's pockets."

Moving on down the body, the Spanish jelly roll known as *brazo de gitano,* or "gypsy's arm," is about the same size and shape as a human forearm. In Lebanon, the long, rolled pastry known as *zunuud as-sitt* has a name that translates as "woman's upper arms." Then, of course, there's also the bent pasta, *elbow macaroni.*

A less obvious example of a food named after arms is the *pretzel.* When English speakers adopted this salty snack from the Germans in the nineteenth century, they used its German name as well, variously written as *Pretzel* or *Brezel.* Both these names come from the Old High German *brezitella,* itself a derivative of an assumed Medieval Latin word, *brāchitellum,* which means "little arm" or "little branch." The reason is that like many other foods that are shaped or marked to signify some religious idea, these twisted biscuits were supposedly designed by European monks as symbols of arms obediently folded in prayer. Thus, the English *pretzel* and German *Brezel* belong to a family of "arm" words, including *embrace* and *bracelet,* as well as *brace,* which is used to support something much as a pair of arms does.

Hands and fingers inspired several food words, such as the name of those long, oval-shaped sponge cakes, *ladyfingers.* In England, by the way, ladyfingers also go by the name *boudoir biscuits.* (*Boudoir* is an intriguing word: borrowed whole from French, this term for "a woman's private sitting room or bedroom" comes from the Old French *bouder,* meaning "to sulk," and originally denoted the private room—of either sex—where presumably sulking occurred.) The term *ladyfingers*, at any rate, sometimes applies to an entirely different food—the elegant, tapering pods of the okra plant. (The word *okra* itself is one of several English food words, including *yam* and *goober*, that derive from African languages.) Australians, however, commonly apply the term *ladyfingers* to bananas—which isn't all that surprising, since in English, a bunch of bananas is also called a "hand."

Another "finger food" is the *date*, which, like fingers, grows from a palm. The ancient Romans, in fact, referred to the flat of the human hand as a *palma* and later applied the same word to the tree whose leaves resemble an oversized version of the same.[2] Like the Greeks, the Romans also noted a resemblance between their own fingers and the palm's smooth, brown, elongated fruit, which they called a *dactylus*, or "finger." The outlines of

---

[2] Speaking of dates and palms, from the Hindi word for "palm tree" derives the name of a beverage known as *tārī* in Hindi, a powerful, intoxicating drink of fermented palm-tree sap. British colonialists in India adopted this term and—presumably after several glasses of *tārī*—began slurring its name in various ways, producing *tarrie, terry, taree, Ztadie, taddy*. They eventually settled on *toddy*, which now applies to a hot drink made with whiskey and sugar. (From the Arabic for "fermented date juice," *'araq at-tamr*, came *arrack*, the name of a fiery Middle Eastern liquor. The Arabic for "date of India," or *tamr hindī*, yielded the name of the tropical fruit commonly used in chutney, curry, and soft drinks, *tamarind*. And these words' Hebrew relative *tamar*, or "date palm," is the source of the feminine names *Tamar* and *Tamara*.)

this ancient word remain visible in the English term *dactyl*, which denotes a metrical pattern in poetry consisting of one long syllable followed by two short ones, the pattern being comparable with that of the bones in a human finger—one long, two short. *Dactylus* also appears in the name of the "wing-fingered" *pterodactyl*. (The *ptero-*, or "wing," in *pterodactyl* also flutters inside the name of that helical-winged machine, a *helicopter*.) Over the centuries, the Romans' name for this "finger-shaped" fruit mutated from *dactylus* into the Old French *date*. The English, in turn, adopted this word whole as a replacement for this fruit's less erudite-sounding Anglo-Saxon name, *fingeraepla*, or "finger-apple."[3]

The *dactyl*, or "finger," lurking inside the English word *date* also appears in the scientific name of the fruit commonly known as *Buddha's hand*. This spectacularly ugly fruit, which resembles a fist of fleshy fingers, is known to botanists as *Citrus media sarcodactylis*. (The *sarco-* in the name comes from the Greek for "flesh" and is the source of such words as *sarcoma*, literally "cancer of the flesh," and *sarcophagus*, literally "flesh-eating," a name applied to stones hollowed out and used for coffins.) All of which brings us to a final finger food,

---

[3] The "finger food" called a date, by the way, is linguistically unrelated to the date on a calendar. The latter arose instead from the Latin for "given," datum, a relative of such "giving" words as donate and donor. Roman letter writers indicated the date by jotting the formulaic phrase "Data Romae"—literally, "given [or issued] at Rome"—followed by a notation of whatever day it happened to be.

dooie vingers, a Dutch recipe for cooked kohlrabi. The pale appearance of these long stalks inspired the name of this dish, which literally means "dead fingers."

Returning to the front of the body, several foods commemorate breasts, nipples, bellies, and navels. Spaniards affectionately call hunks of a famous cheese from Galicia *tetillas,* or "little tits," because of their inviting shape. The Turkish pastry *kadin gobegi* has a name that describes its appearance, for it resembles a "woman's belly button." Then there are *navel oranges,* which look as if they have one. As we'll see in the next chapter, many other foods allude suggestively to the chests and torsos of various religious or mythical figures, including *nun's tummies, Venus's breasts, St. Agatha's nipples,* and *sacred navels.*

Below-the-waist body parts appear in various food names as well: the Aztecs, for example, applied their word for "testicle," *ahuacatl,* to a favorite fleshy fruit with a similar shape. Spanish conquistadors who later encountered this unfamiliar green delicacy appropriated this name but modified it to one that sounded more familiar and felt more comfortable on the Spanish tongue: *aguacate,* which in English became *avocado.* Similarly, the Aztecs added their word *molli,* or "sauce," to the name of the *ahuacatl* to form the name of the greenish mixture they made from mashing up this testicle-shaped fruit; again, Spaniards borrowed the sauce-word *ahuacamolli,* but then altered it to *guacamole.*

As the inimitable food writer Jay Jacobs has noted, the Swahili term *pili-pili,* which denotes an extremely hot capsicum pepper, is also slang for "penis." The same double meaning is present in the Korean pepper name *golchu,* and in Louisiana and east Texas another piquant pod with a similarly suggestive shape goes by the not unsurprising name *peter pepper.*

Whether the English pudding *spotted dick* belongs in this category is a matter of some debate. As John Ayto notes in his delightful book *The Glutton's Glossary,* this food's name "has made it the target of double entendres as leaden as the pudding itself often is." According to the *Oxford English Dictionary,* the word *dick* was being used to mean "plain pudding" for almost a decade before the first recorded citation of *dick* as vulgar slang for "penis" in 1891. Even before that, *dick* served as both a dialectal word for "a kind of hard cheese" and a word for "riding whip." (As the *OED* helpfully explains, a "gold-headed dick"—in the sense of "riding whip"—was "one so ornamented.") Of course, it's unclear how long the vulgar slang use of the term was in circulation before it was actually recorded.

Continuing on down the body, some foods have legs in their names. The Pennsylvania Dutch stew of beef with potato dumplings called *boova shenkel* translates as "boy's legs," a reference to the dumplings' shape. The Turkish entrée *kadinbudu koefte* has a name that translates as "women's-thigh meatballs." In Bavaria, "kneecap cookies," or *Kniekuchle,* are deep-fried yeast cakes similar to doughnuts, except that they're stretched as thinly as possible in the middle without making a hole. This name apparently has been reinforced by the fact that Bavarian cooks are said to press such cakes over their own kneecaps in order to achieve just the right shape and thinness. And in France, the round, flat, edible mollusk known as a *patelle* gets its name from the Latin word for "kneecap," *patella*.

A toe pokes out of the German name for "a clove of garlic," *Knoblauchzehe*, or "garlic toe." (Spaniards, however, pull off a "tooth," or *diente*, from a "head," or *cabeza*, of garlic.) In Brazil, a popular peanut brittle is jokingly called *pé-de-moleque*, or, roughly translated, "naughty children's toes." Another foot word that may appear at a meal: *bain-de-pied*, or "footbath," which denotes excess coffee that spills out from a cup and onto the saucer when poured. Then there are the various types of flatfish called *sole:* Like the *sole* on the bottom of one's foot, they derive their name from the Latin *solea*, which originally meant "sandal."

Buns? No. Although the source of the name for these baked goods is not entirely clear, some authorities suspect it comes from an Old French word, *bugne*, meaning "a bump on the head" or "a boil." (Similarly, the puffy New Orleans doughnut-without-a-hole known as a *beignet* may be related to a group of words pertaining to "bumps" and "bruises," including the painful swelling on a foot known as a *bunion*.) And even though the buns on one's backside may resemble the doughy kind, the name of this body part is thought to come instead from a Scottish Gaelic term, *bun*, "the hind part of a rabbit or squirrel," which may also be the source of *bunny*.

In any case, one of the most picturesque food names referring to body parts is the one for a mixture of string beans and navy beans popular in the Netherlands. Hardly known for their prudishness, the Dutch fondly refer to this dish as *blote billetjes in het gras*, or "bare buttocks in the grass."

Foods That Look Like Animals

Dig into a plateful of *vermicelli*, and you're dining on "little worms" — at least from an etymological point of view. The source of this picturesque pasta name is the Latin word *vermis*, or "worm," which wriggled into several other English words as well. There's *worm* itself, not to mention that "worm-shaped" hanger-on known as the *vermiform* appendix, *vermiculture* or "earthworm farming," and *vermilion*, a red dye formerly made from the dried, wormy-looking bodies of insect larvae. These worm words are also related to *vermin*, a word which, as the *OED* relates, originally applied to "reptiles, stealthy or slinking animals" and only later came to indicate other types of creatures. (At least two other vermiform creatures have burrowed into notable English words. The word *bombastic*, which describes inappropriately lofty or "padded" language, comes from the Greek *bombyx*, or "silkworm," a creature known for producing material suitable for padding. Similarly, the name of the fluffy-ribbed fabric *chenille* was borrowed intact from a French word that means "hairy caterpillar." And speaking of caterpillars, the Italian pasta called *bozzoli* has a name that literally means "cocoons," for reasons that become abundantly clear when you see a plateful of them.)

A snake lurks on many a dining table in the form of an *aspic,* the name of which supposedly comes from the French *aspic,* or "asp." Etymologists disagree about exactly why this jellied mold should conjure up images of a venomous reptile. Some argue that the name refers to the colors of aspics, which vary like a snakeskin's. Others contend that its name stems from the fact that this food is cold to the touch, as in the proverbial French expression *froid comme un aspic,* or "cold as an asp." A meal that features an aspic might be appropriately topped off with a serving of the coiled German pastry called a *Schnecke,* which is a linguistic relative of and has the same meaning as the English *snail.*

Insects buzz inside a few other food names as well, including, oddly enough, *lobster,* which is thought to derive from the Latin word for "locust." When speakers of Old English were casting about for a name for this crustacean, they borrowed the Latin *locusta* and altered it to *loppestre,* a word perhaps also influenced by the Old English word *loppe,* or "spider." High-fiber breakfast cereals that include the seeds known as *psyllium,* meanwhile, have a case of fleas, linguistically speaking. This natural laxative takes its name from the Greek word *psulla,* or "flea," because its tiny seeds swell and become gelatinous when moist. More appetizing, perhaps, are the pasta known as *farfalle,* or "butterflies," because of their double-winged shape.[4] Then there's the British cookie called a *garibaldi*, after the nineteenth-century Italian nationalist leader Giuseppe Garibaldi; it contains a layer of currants inside, which is why it's also known as a *squashed-fly biscuit*, or in Scotland, a *fly's graveyard*.

Incidentally, a fancied resemblance between the smell of bedbugs and that of *coriander* may be the source of this fragrant herb's name. That, at least, was the belief of ancient writers, who pointed out a connection between the spice's Greek name, *koriandron*, and the Greek word for "bedbug," *koris*. (If true, this would also make *coriander* a linguistic relative of the flower *coreopsis*, whose name literally means "bedbuglike." The reason: the tiny, horned seeds of this yellow flower look like little insects with antennae—which is why this flower also goes by the name *tickseed*.)

Bird words inspired several other dishes, including *spätzle*, the German noodles whose name translates as "little sparrows." Spanish speakers sometimes refer to popcorn with the endearing name *palomitas*, or "little doves," *palomitas* being a linguistic relative of the feminine name *Paloma*, or "dove," as well as the word for a "dove-colored" horse, *palomino*.

---

[4] Another butterfly word sometimes appearing in kitchens is *papillote*, the name of the frilly little paper hat that is sometimes stuck on the end of a cutlet bone. It comes from the French for "butterfly," *papillon*, and is a linguistic relative of what was originally a large, "winged" tent, a *pavilion*. (Incidentally, in case you were wondering which Central American country takes its name for a native word for "butterfly," it's *Panamá*.)

In Sweden, a fancied resemblance between geese and lumps of butter led to the Swedish dialectal term *gås*, or "butter," from an Old Norse word meaning "goose." The image of these bird-shaped butterballs later found its way into the Swedish term *smörgås*, meaning "bread and butter" or "open-face sandwich"—a term which, when added to the Swedish word *bord*, or "table," formed *smörgåsbord*, the classic Swedish feast featuring a table spread with such sandwiches and assorted delicacies. Sweden's neighbors to the south later anglicized this word with a bird in it and now apply it broadly to mean a "plentiful collection of various things."

As improbable as it sounds, the dessert known as a *pie* may be yet another food with a name inspired by a bird. In this case, it's the *magpie*, sometimes called simply a *pie*. This feathered creature's name is a combination of the feminine name *Mag* (a nickname for *Margaret*, proverbially applied to notorious chatterers) and *pica*, this bird's Latin name. Some lexicographers argue convincingly that the connection between the feathered pie and the flaky one hinges on the fact that a pie tends to be filled with a variety of things. One hypothesis is that the pie's miscellaneous innards recall the bird's notorious habit of collecting various and sundry items and hoarding them in its nest. Such an explanation may sound far-fetched, but it's strengthened by the fact that the name of the Scottish specialty *haggis*—a boiled sheep's stomach stuffed with the minced organs of a sheep or calf mixed with onions, oatmeal, and seasonings—is quite similar to the obsolete English *haggess* or *haggiss*, which, as it happens, means "magpie." According to another explanation, the baked type of *pie*'s name refers to the way its jumbled contents resemble a magpie's splotchy, *piebald* plumage.

Parts of birds also show up in various foods. The short, diagonally cut tubes of Italian pasta called *penne* take their name from Latin *penna*, which means "feather" and, by extension, "quill pen." *Penne* is part of the etymological flock that includes *pen* (the writing kind) and *panache*, which was first borrowed into English from French in the mid–sixteenth century to denote "a plume of feathers atop a helmet" or "a tuft of feathers used as a headdress." By the turn of the century, *panache* had acquired its current sense of "flamboyance," "verve," and "swaggering display." In fact, the English word *panached* is applied to describe anything striped like a feather — tulips, for example — while its French cousin *glace panachée* denotes ice cream that is similarly striped.

Although well camouflaged, another bird word nests inside in the cookery term *beef olive*, which in fact isn't an olive at all but rather thick slices of beef rolled with onions and herbs and stewed in a brown sauce. According to John Ayto's *The Glutton's Glossary*, the *olive* in a *beef olive* is an alteration of the Old French *alou*, or "lark," as in the modern French *alouette* of children's-song fame. These rolls of meat are so called, Ayto explains, "on account of their supposed resemblance to small birds, particularly headless ones prepared for the table." Although the standard French word for this dish is *paupiettes* — a descendant of the Latin *pulpa,* or "pulp" — they're also known as *alouettes sans têtes,* literally, "larks without heads," or *oiseaux sans têtes,* "birds without heads." The *oiseaux,* or "birds," in the latter expression arose from the Latin *avis,* or "bird," which also hatched such words as *aviary* and *aviation.* In Poland, meanwhile, a stuffed cabbage is a "little pigeon," or *golumpki.* Birds don't fare much better in the Netherlands, where the name *blinde vinken,* literally "blind finches," is applied to meat loaf wrapped in bacon. Birds are also oddly absent from the specialty that Venetians playfully call *polenta e oseleti scapai.* This plateful of miscellaneous ingredients and cornmeal has a name that literally means "polenta and little birds that got away."

Dutch diners also sup on small bits of fried meat or fish that are called *papagaaien tongen,* or "parrots' tongues," while in Arabic, the little rice-shaped pasta otherwise known as orzo goes by the descriptive but rather grisly name *lisaan al-'asfuur,* or "birds' tongues." (The name *orzo,* on the other hand, is actually an Italian word for "barley," the pasta being named for its resemblance to little grains thereof.) In ancient China, cloves were called *ki she kiang,* or "bird's-tongue spice," because of a resemblance between the two.

The roundness of a bird's eye inspired the name of a tiny round Italian pasta called *occhi di passeri,* or "sparrows' eyes," the *passeri* being a relative of the English adjective *passerine,* or "sparrowlike." The same image appears in the name of the tiny red or green pods that impart a fiery flavor to many Thai dishes, *bird's-eye chilis*. A rooster's beak, meanwhile, pokes through the name of the piquant Mexican sauce *pico de gallo*, and the pasta known as *creste di gallo* has an Italian name indicating that it's shaped like a "rooster's comb." *Gooseneck squash* lives up to its name, sporting a dramatically coiled neck resembling that of the big, honking birds. And the English cider apple called a *coccagee* takes its name from the Irish *cac a' ghéidh*—literally, "turd of goose"—inspired by the fruit's greenish-yellow color.

Bird's-nest soup literally refers to its contents, of course, which include nests of an Asian bird constructed with the animal's own gelatinous spit. But more fanciful references to nests appear in cookbooks as well. In the Netherlands, the name *Vogelnestjes*, or "birds' nests," denotes meatballs containing an egg, while *Zwaluwnestjes*, or "swallows' nests," are schnitzels with an egg inside. And in New England, a thick-crusted, deep-dish pie goes by the name *bird's-nest pudding* or *crow's-nest pudding*.

Other members of the animal world are represented in various Mexican-American dishes. The *burrito*, or "little donkey," was perhaps named because its curved surface resembles the back of one or because it is laden with many ingredients, like a beast of burden. The origin of *chimichanga*, the name of a deep-fried burrito, is subject to much debate, but one intriguing possibility appears in *The Dictionary of American Food and Drink*, which notes rather cryptically that in Spanish the word *changa* means "female monkey" and *chimenea* means "chimney or hearth." When put together, these words become an "unmentionable expletive that mentions a monkey." This might lend credence to stories circulating throughout the Southwest that the first of these crispy creations was invented when a cook accidentally knocked a burrito into a deep-fat fryer and shouted, "*Chimichanga!*"

Tex-Mex enthusiasts also munch on *ratitos*, or "little rats," a playful name for fried, stuffed jalapeño peppers with their stems intact. Linguistically speaking, an appropriate accompaniment for a plateful of these appetizers would be the tiny but red-hot Thai chilies called *prik khee noo*, literally, "rat droppings." "Little mice" also scurried into the name of the Dutch confection of sugared caraway seeds, *muisjes*. And the French have a most evocative name for the fuzzy brown fruits from New Zealand commonly called *kiwis;* in France, they're *souris végétales*, or "vegetable mice."

Ungulates, or "hoofed" animals — or parts thereof — have moseyed into our culinary vocabulary as well.[5] The edible flower called *bugloss* takes its name from the

---

[5] *Ungulate*, by the way, comes from the Latin *unguis*, meaning "nail," "claw," or "hoof," and is therefore a linguistic cousin of the English word *nail*. Both these words are also related to *onyx*, a deliciously picturesque name that comes from a kindred Greek word for "fingernail," *onux*, because the pink-and-white variety of onyx very much resembles the color of a human fingernail.

Greek for "ox tongue," because its leaves have a similar shape and roughness. The *bu-* in *bugloss* is a relative of *butter, bovine,* and *bulimia* (literally, "ox hunger"), and the *-gloss,* or "tongue," in its name sticks out of such words as *glossary* and *glossalalia,* or "speaking in tongues." The Mediterranean fish called a *boops,* often used in bouillabaisse, has a name that translates from the Greek as "cow-eyed," the *-ops* in its name being kin to such "eye" words as *optical* and *ophthalmologist.* The name of another bovine body part, *bullock's heart,* is applied to a large, ribbed apple also known as the *costard,* which can weigh up to ten pounds. (In English, by the way, the three-syllable word *boopic* is a useful but rarely used word meaning "ox-eyed.")

The mild, slightly salty Italian cheese called *caciocavallo* is sometimes mistakenly assumed to come from mare's milk, since its name appears to translate as "horse cheese." Actually, however, *caciocavallo* is so called because it's molded into large gourdlike shapes, then set across a framework of sticks to dry, as if astride a little horse. And Italians fondly bestowed the name *porcini,* or "little pigs," on a variety of plump mushrooms that can weigh up to a pound each.

The bristly *hedgehog* has a place in the dining room as well. A 1723 cookbook offered the following instructions for making a dish by that name: "Almonds, . . . Eggs, . . . Cream, . . . Butter, . . . stirring, till it is stiff enough to be made in the Form of a Hedge-hog; then stick it full of blanch'd Almonds, . . . like the Bristles of

25

a Hedge-hog." The same name has been used for the clove-studded whole orange that's a key ingredient in a punch bowl full of the hot wine drink called *bishop* (more about which can be found in Chapter 2).

Cats creep into the vocabulary of the kitchen in the form of the thin, flat, and variously flavored French biscuits *langues de chat,* or "cats' tongues." In the slang of lunch-counter and coffee-shop workers, the phrase *cat's eyes* denotes the beady pudding tapioca, made from the starchy cassava root, an important food source in South America. (*Tapioca* itself has an uninspiring pedigree; it comes from a term used by indigenous peoples of Brazil to mean "squeeze out the dregs.") *Cat's-head biscuits* are a southern U.S. specialty, jocularly named for their resemblance in size and shape to the head of a tabby. The sound of caterwauling felines also apparently inspired the eerily named German dish of boiled meat, onion, and eggs all fried together called *Katzag-'schrei,* or "cats screaming."

Not surprisingly, dogs have also left their linguistic mark in the kitchen. *Rollmops,* those highly spiced, marinated filets of herring wrapped around a gherkin or onion and secured with a stick, are one such food. Because they're short and stubby, the name of these hors d'oeuvres derives from the German *rollen,* meaning "to roll," and *Mops,* which means "pug dog." (Although the word *rollmops* is often misunderstood as a plural, the German *Mops* in the latter half of this name means that technically just one of these is still a *rollmops.* In any case, one or more rollmops are supposedly good for hangovers—even if they don't contain any hair of the dog.)

In Britain, the name of the pudding *spotted dick* is sometimes mercifully euphemized as *spotted dog*. The Brits also faithfully consume *dog-in-a-blanket*, a jam pudding or rolled currant dumpling, not to be confused with *toad-in-the-hole*, or sausage in batter. Meanwhile, the deep-fried cornmeal dumplings known as *hush puppies*, long popular in the southern United States, supposedly got their name from the practice of tossing scraps of them to barking dogs to make them stop. And in the Netherlands, a Dutch version of what Americans call *French toast* is sometimes affectionately known as *wentelteefjes*, which, politely translated, means "female dogs rolling over."

The French apply the name *cul de chien*, literally, "dog's ass," to the apple-shaped fruit called the medlar, which is distinguished by the way it puckers suggestively at one end. (In fact, this same fruit sometimes goes by the English name *open arse*, because of its likeness to a vulva. Shakespeare plays upon this sense in *Romeo and Juliet*, when Mercutio observes of the lovesick swain: "Now he will sit under a medlar tree, / And wish his mistress were that kind of fruit / As maids call medlars, when they laugh alone. / O, Romeo, that she were, O that she were / An open-arse, thou a pop'rin pear"—pop'rin pears being a phallic-looking fruit from Belgium.) The dog's cousin, the wolf, meanwhile, snarls inside a French term for "sandwich bread cut into triangles," *dent-de-loup*, or "wolf's tooth."

Foods That Look Like Clothes

The names of quite a few foods suggest they are wearable. Head coverings, for example, inspired the names of such foods as *cappelletti,* the little hat-shaped pasta, as well as those blazingly hot peppers, *Scotch bonnets.* There's also *roomali roti,* a popular bread in India that's as thin as the "scarf" for which it's named. And, of course, there's *bow-tie pasta.*

From the Latin *manica,* or "sleeve," comes the Italian name for those roomy, stuffable sleeves of pasta, *manicotti.* Both of these words belong to a venerable family of words having to do with "hands," including *manual, manicure, manipulate, manufacture,* and *manuscript,* the last two of which don't always live up to their original sense of making or writing something "by hand." These "hand" terms are also kin to *manqué,* which describes someone who fails to reach his or her ambitions, such as a *singer manqué.* Borrowed into English from French, *manqué* comes from the Latin "hand" word *mancus,* which the Romans used to describe someone who was "maimed (particularly in the hand)."

One French cake, in fact, now goes by the name *manqué.* The story goes that a famous Parisian baker was once preparing a pastry made with egg whites that were badly whisked and lumpy. The baker's boss exclaimed, "The cake is a failure!," or "*Le gâteau est manqué!*" Nevertheless, the frugal baker turned his failure into a success by adding butter and topping the cake with pralines. A customer immediately bought it, loved it, and returned several days later for another and asked what it was called. The baker shrugged his shoulders and told her it was a *manqué*, but he could certainly make another.

Other wearable foods include *ditali* and its miniature version, *ditalini*, the small pieces of pasta whose names come from the Italian for "thimble" or "finger of a glove." These names are the etymological kin of "finger" words in several other languages, including the Greek *dactylos*, the English *digit*, and their French and Spanish cognates, *doigt* and *dedo*. The pasta called *annelli*, meanwhile, has a name that translates from the Italian as "little rings" and is a linguistic relative of *annular*, which describes an eclipse in which the sun forms a complete ring of light around the heavenly body blocking it. *Annelli* and *annular* are also the etymological kin of the four-letter word denoting a commonly invoked ringlike sphincter.

From the Italian for "trouser leg" comes the name of the little stuffed pizza known as *calzone*. In the Netherlands, a square almond-and-egg-white pastry goes by the name *luier*, or "diaper." Still other foods in that country are named for fashion accessories, such as the long green beans the Dutch call *kouseband*, or "garters." (The same folks refer to French green beans as *prikkeldraad*, or "barbed wire.") From the Italian *tagliare*, "to cut"—a relative of the English *tailor*—comes the pasta name *tagliatelli*, or "little ribbons." The noodles called *fettuccine* also have a name that means "ribbons," apparently a descendant of the Italian *fetta,* or "slice." From the Italian *fetta* also comes the name of a Greek "cheese," or *turi,* called *turi pheta* — a "slice" of cheese better known to speakers of English as *feta* cheese.

Moving on through the etymological closet, the Swiss have a sort of apple dumpling they call *Apfel im Schlafrock,* or "apple in its bathrobe." The French for "apple turnover," meanwhile, is *chausson aux pommes,* literally, "apple sock."[6] The Louisiana shortbread known as *petticoat tails,* a recipe brought to America by Scottish immigrants, is often baked in specially shaped molds resembling the sweeping shapes of such undergarments. Their name, however, more likely arises from the Scots' adaptation of an Old French expression for "little cakes," *petits gastels.*

Another familiar food name was inspired, if only indirectly, by a pair of shoes: *Twinkies.* When the inventor of these spongy, creme-filled cakes was trying to think of a name for his new product, he chanced upon a billboard ad in Saint Louis promoting "Twinkle Toe Shoes." James Dewar was so taken with this name that he decided to adapt it — presumably not because his new cre-

---

[6] Interestingly enough, several languages use various food names to denote a "hole in a sock through which the flesh protrudes." Spaniards refer to it as a *tomate,* or "tomato," while the Dutch call it a *knol,* or "turnip." For the past hundred years or so, the OED says, English speakers have dubbed the same fleshy bulge a "potato."

ations resembled shoes or tasted like air-sole inserts, but simply because he liked the sound of the word.[7]

Then there's the Cuban dish of flank steak simmered with onions, green peppers, and garlic called *ropa vieja.* The meat is cooked all day long and then shredded, and the miscellaneous nature of the resulting mixture inspired this hearty food's name, which in Spanish means "old clothes." (Another, more grisly explanation for the name, however, is that it refers to the practice of curing large slabs of goat meat to be used in the dish by hanging it from clotheslines.)

Foods That Look Like Miscellaneous Objects

Many other culinary terms preserve the names of miscellaneous items, from furniture to musical instruments

---

[7] Strangely enough, this wasn't the only time a chance glance at an ad for shoes inspired a well-known culinary trademark. In 1876, at a time when most ketchup was homemade, German-American chef and entrepreneur Henry Heinz created the first mass-produced ketchup, which he called Heinz Tomato Catsup and advertised as "Blessed relief for Mother and the other women in the household!" His highly successful company soon expanded to include a long line of products from fruit butters to pickle relish. Several years later, the story goes, Heinz was riding an elevated train in New York when he happened to see a sign above a store advertising "21 Styles of Shoes." Turning that idea over in his mind several times, he came up with a catchphrase for his own company: "57 Varieties," now familiar to millions as part of the label on bottles of *Heinz 57.*

to grass. For example, in French, a *canapé* is literally a "couch," and the edible kind is a piece of bread or toast upon which other savories sit. The linguistic history of *canapé* is surprising. This word for "couch" goes all the way back to the Greek term *kōnōps*, meaning "gnat" or "mosquito." The connection between the two is this: From *kōnōps* came the Greek *kōnōpion*, a word designating a type of "bed or couch surrounded by curtains to keep away mosquitoes." Over the centuries this word evolved into terms in various languages for gauzy mosquito netting hung around beds and couches, and these names in turn eventually gave rise to words denoting the couch itself—as well as the modern English word *canopy*.

Other foods that are named for their resemblances to musical instruments: *Flautas*, tortillas that are rolled around meat filling and then fried in oil, are so named because of their resemblance to a "flute." *Timbales*, from the French for "kettledrums," are various dishes of meat, vegetables, or fish smothered in a creamy sauce and baked in a drum-shaped mold. Such foods might be best served with the crisp, flat Sardinian bread *carta da musica*, whose name means "sheet music." (In many kitchens, an echo of another musical instrument is audible: the slicing device called a *mandoline* is so named because some types resemble a mandolin.)

Still other edibles are named for various miscellaneous objects. *Sigara boelgi* is a rolled-up Turkish treat of phyllo dough and meat, cheese, or spinach, and indeed it looks like a cigar. In Mexico, the word *taco* refers to a tortilla rolled around a filling of meat or cheese; the name is said to come from the Spanish for "billiard cue." The Tex-Mex adaptation of this food is the crisp-fried and filled *taco shell*, which bears more of a resemblance to *taco*'s alternate meanings in Spanish — "plug" or "wad of bank notes."

Plants have inspired several food names. The Italian pasta *gramigna* gets its name from an imagined resemblance to blades of "grass," sharing an etymological ancestor with English *graminous* and *graminivorous*, which mean "grassy" and "grass-eating." Although no one knows for sure how *strawberries* were named, some etymologists conjecture that it's because their red surface is flecked with little straw-colored particles, or possibly because the plant's runners resemble straw. (Similarly, *runner beans* are named for the "runners," or creeping stems, they send out.) The exceedingly thin pastry dough called *phyllo* gets its name from the Greek word for "leaf." Similarly, the name of the *mille-feuille*, the many-layered puff-pastry cake, is French for "thousand leaf." Both these names stem from a family of leafy words, including *foliage, folio, foil*, and *chlorophyll* (literally, "green leaf").

Other plant words whose outlines are visible in food names include the Latin *calamus*, or "reed," a possible source of the name of the sweet result of heating sugar cane, *caramel*. In ancient Rome, *calamus* soon extended not only to mean "reed" but to indicate the writing instrument made from one. Many scholars believe that in turn this word may have given us the Italian *calamari,* or "squid," because of either this creature's pen-shaped internal shell or, perhaps more likely, the fact that it squirts ink. Speaking of long, thin plant parts, the Latin word for "stick," *baculum,* gave us the name of the long, sticklike French bread known as a *baguette* as well as the name of the stick-shaped microscopic organism called a *bacillus,* a relative also of the Greek *bacterium* — literally, "little stick."[8]

Boats float within other edibles' names. Spanish *chalupas,* or "boats," are fried corn tortillas shaped into hulls and then loaded with a culinary cargo of vegetables, cheese, or meat. (*Chalupa* is an etymological cousin of the English word for the type of boat known as a *shallop.*) *Barquettes,* likewise, are hors d'oeuvres holders shaped like "little boats," their French name sharing a common source with such seagoing words as the English *barge* and *bark,* as in those "Nicean barks of yore" in Edgar Allan Poe's poem "To Helen." (Presumably neither *chalupas* nor *barquettes* should be served anywhere near *Strudel,* which in German means "whirlpool.")

Food names that reflect the elements include *oeufs à la neige,* or "snowlike eggs" (whipped egg whites

---

[8] A picturesque linguistic cousin of these "stick" words is *debacle.* It comes from the French *débâcler,* meaning "to remove a bar." In the early nineteenth century *débâcler* specified "to break up ice in a river," which led to a "sudden deluge or violent rush of water." Only later did the word come to be associated more abstractly with a "sudden fragmenting or downfall" or "stampede."

poached and served atop egg custard), and *neige de Florence,* or "Florentine snow," which features flakes of extremely delicate, pure-white pasta dropped into clear soups. Various frothy, chilled desserts of egg whites, gelatin, and flavorings go by such names as *apple snow* or *lemon snow.* Then of course, there are *snow cones.* The name of the Dutch mishmash of cooked apples, potatoes, and bacon, *hete bliksem,* literally means "hot lightning," *bliksem* being related to *blitz*—as in the German *Blitzkrieg,* or "lightning war"—and *Blitzen,* whose name Santa traditionally calls after that of his four-hoofed colleague *Donner,* whose name means "thunder" in German.

The French word for "lightning," meanwhile, flashes within the name of that heavenly pastry the *éclair.* No one's exactly sure why, but some surmise that this name refers to the gleam of its icing, or to the baker's admonition that these pastries be whisked out of the oven and served "in a flash." (Whatever the reason, this pastry's name is a close relative of several other "bright," "clear" words, including *clear, clairvoyant, claret,* and *éclaircissement,* the last of these being a fancy word for "explanation.") Then there's the North Carolina specialty known as a *zephrina.* Like the English word *zephyr,* the name of this light, airy cookie comes from a Greek word for "wind."

Finally, some foods resemble weapons. Due to the long, pointed shape of its leaves, the name of the pungent herb *garlic* comes from two Old English words that literally mean "spear-leek." The *gar-* in its name is related to a whole slew of slaying names, including *Gertrude*, literally, "strong spear." There's also *Gerald* ("spear rule"), *Gerard* ("spear brave"), *Garrett* ("spear mighty"), *Garibaldi* ("spear bold"), and *Roger* ("famous spear"). Meanwhile, the earliest version of the dessert called a *bombe* featured layers of ice cream or sherbet frozen into a spherical mold. Similarly, the voluptuously rounded *papaya* fruit goes by the name *fruta bomba* in Spanish. Incidentally, the diminutive of Spanish *bomba* is *bombilla*, which, picturesquely enough, means "lightbulb."

It's worth noting that in Germany a "lightbulb" goes by the charming name *Glühbirne*, literally, "glow-pear," or simply *Birne*, "pear." In fact, just as many food words arose from the names of everyday objects, a surprising number of everyday English words arose from other terms involving food and drink—just as the German word for "pear" gave rise to a common term for "lightbulb." In fact, many English words, such as *lady, lampoon, garble,* and *galaxy* contain similarly picturesque images of food and drink. We'll meet many more of them in Chapter 6.

2

ANGEL'S HAIR, DEVIL'S DROPPINGS, NUN'S TUMMIES, AND MONK'S BALLS

Food Names Associated with Religion and the Supernatural

When a person dies, Germans say that "He has put aside his spoon"—*Er hat den Löffel abgegeben.* Spanish speakers sometimes say that someone newly deceased *dobló la servilleta,* or "folded her napkin." In China, friends greet each other not by inquiring after their health or asking how they "are," but instead saying *"Chi le ma?,"* or "Have you eaten today?"

As these idioms suggest, the difference between eating and not eating is, of course, the difference between life and death. This most fundamental of mysteries—the miraculous transformation of food into flesh and into food once more—has always proved irresistible to the human imagination. So it's hardly surprising that food and drink should be intimately connected with that which seeks to address these ultimate questions of life and death—namely, religion. Water into wine, bread into flesh, knowledge in a bite of fruit, immortality in a cup . . . these and other images of eating and drinking pervade religious ritual, tradition, and scripture.

The reverse is also true: religious imagery appears within myriad words for various foods and beverages. Some of those names apparently were bestowed reverently, as in those foods that commemorate religious holidays or honor a beloved saint. But a surprising number of divinely inspired food words are quite humorous. Many, for example, reflect a naughty delight in caricaturing men and women of the cloth, while others poke fun at the hypocrisy of the falsely pious. Still other food words reflect a certain wistfulness about immortality and the tantalizing hope that putting aside one's spoon or folding one's napkin for the final time really isn't the end after all.

We'll begin by looking at foods that commemorate those ethereal errand runners, the angels, then move on to foods whose names recall their diabolical counterparts.

Angels and Devils

In any discussion of foods with religious-sounding name, the airy white dessert known as *angel's food cake* or *angel-food cake* quickly comes to mind. But long ago, speakers of English used the term *angel's food* to denote a kind of strong ale. *Angel food* is also slang for the obligatory sermon following a free meal at the Salvation Army or some other evangelical mission. (*Evangelical,* by the way, is a close etymological relative of the *angel* in *angel food,* both words coming from the Greek *angelos,* or "messenger." Add *angelos* to the Greek word *eu,* or "good," as in *euthanasia,* or "good death," and the result is *euangelos,* the forerunner of the English word for the *evangelist*—someone who literally claims to bear "good news.")

These divinely dispatched beings also inspired the name of a Swedish dessert made with whipped cream, lingonberry jam, and cake crumbs called *anglamat,* or "angel food." This Scandinavian treat may be the inspiration for the baked meringue shell filled with similar ingredients that Americans call *angel pie. Angel bread,* meanwhile, is a high-fiber cake made from oatmeal, flour, ginger, and the cathartic plant called *spurge* (a linguistic cousin of *purge* and *expurgate*), which is said to be helpful as a laxative. Another herb that supposedly confers medicinal blessings is *angelica,* from the Medieval Latin *herba angelica,* or "angelic herb," which is also a key ingredient in the dessert wine *angeliquor.*

Parts of angels are also visible in the names of foods. The extremely thin noodles known as *capelli d'angelo* are supposedly as fine as "angel's hair." Inhabitants of the isle of Majorca enjoy an even sweeter version of "angel hair": caramelized strands of spaghetti squash called *cabello de ángel*. In southern France, *cheveux d'ange*, or "angel hair," denotes a dish made of julienned carrots that are boiled with sugar, lemon, and vanilla.

Angels also manifest themselves in the form of the bacon-wrapped cooked oysters served on buttered toast points known as *angels on horseback*, a direct translation of the French *anges à cheval* (a *chevalier* in French being a "horseman"). Diners in Portugal nibble on *papos de anjo*, or "angel's breasts," a heavenly dessert that is similarly shaped. In the United States, however, an *angel teat* is a shot of mellow whiskey. Ask a bartender for an *angel's kiss*, though, and you'll get a cocktail of crème de cacao, cream, and brandies or liqueurs gently poured in order of density, so that this drink's contrasting ingredients form an angelic hierarchy of sorts.

At the other end of the spiritual spectrum, many foods' names jokingly invoke the Devil, usually those that are either spicy hot or so tempting as to be sinful. (Not that sin is such a bad thing in these cases. In fact, the compliment every Italian restaurant proprietor hopes to hear is that the meal he or she just served was a *peccato di gola*, or "sin of the throat.") *Devils on horseback*, for example, is much like *angels on horseback*, with the addition of Tabasco sauce or cayenne. To *devil* a mixture of ham or eggs means to throw in some fiery spices. In France, the word *devil*'s cognate, *diable*, is used to describe a piquant sauce of wine, vinegar, and shallots. And in Italy, *pollo alla diavola* is a recipe for spicy, grilled chicken "the way the Devil likes it"—a dish somewhat similar to the one with a deliciously irritable name that in Italian means "angry chicken," *pollo all'arrabbiata.*

A diabolical creature haunts *coconuts,* a word that comes from the Portuguese word for "goblin" or "bogeyman," *coco.* The name alludes to those three indentations at the bottom of a coconut shell that do indeed resemble a spooky little face. (All the more reason to complement a serving of coconut with some *ahole.* Often found on Hawaiian menus, the name of this silvery fish derives from an islanders' expression meaning "to strip away," because this fish is believed to drive away evil spirits.)

A devil also may lurk in a loaf of *pumpernickel* bread. Many etymologists believe that *pumpernickel* comes from the German for "devil fart," the *pumpern-* meaning "to fart" and *-Nickel* meaning "devil, demon, or goblin." The reason is that supposedly this dark bread is coarse enough to produce outbursts of flatulence as powerful as those of the Devil himself. The *-Nickel,* or "devil," in *pumpernickel* also inspired the English word *nickel.* This metallic element was first extracted from a copper-colored ore that German miners dismissed as *Kupfernickel,* literally, "copper devil," because it looks deceptively rich in copper but actually contains very little. The Swiss mineralogist who first isolated this metal from its maligned source christened it with a shortened version of the tricky ore's name, *nickel.*[1] A slice of pumpernickel, at any rate, might be an appropriate accompaniment for the strong French goat cheese called *crottins du diable,* or "devil's droppings."

Finally, there's *devil's food cake,* an American invention that first appeared around 1900, some twenty years after the appearance of angel-food cake. The name *devil's food,* of course, suggests both its sinful richness and the contrast between its dark chocolate color and that of its angelic counterpart.

Saints and Sinners

Images of the religious faithful—as well as a few of the unchurched—appear in many names associated with food and drink. The hot beverage that Samuel Taylor Coleridge called "Spicy bishop, drink divine"—a blend of mulled wine, citrus, sugar, and other spices—is so named because its deep red color resembles that of a

---

[1] Actually, something similar happened with the word *cobalt.* This English term is an adaptation of the element's German name, *Kobalt,* which in turn comes from the German for "goblin" or "demon." The element's mischievous name arose from the fact that originally miners assumed that cobalt was a worthless hindrance to their efforts to dig for silver. Not only that, it seemed to play nasty tricks on their health, like a malicious spirit. In fact, the related English word *kobold* has come to mean "mischievous household elf" or "gnome or spirit that haunts underground caves."

bishop's robes.[2] Mulled red wine sometimes also goes by the name *cardinal,* while a version made with white wine or champagne is called, not surprisingly, *pope.*[3]

At the opposite end of the church hierarchy, a steaming cup of *cappuccino* commemorates the dull gray or brown garb worn by the austere order of monks known as the *Capuchins.* Recognizable by their drab, simple robes topped with a pointed hood, these friars

---

[2] Incidentally, in parts of northern England, the dialectal phrase *to bishop* means "to burn a food while cooking." Current since the 1500s, this expression apparently stems from a proverbial phrase, "The bishop has put his foot into it." The phrase may allude to the penchant among some ecclesiastical officials for burning people at the stake who happened to disagree with their theology. As William Tindale pointed out in the early sixteenth century, "If the porage be burned . . . or the meate ouer rosted, we say the bishop hath put his foote in the potte, or the bishop hath played the cooke, because the bishops burn who they lust and whosoever displeaseth them." John Milton used this expression, as did Jonathan Swift when he wrote in 1738, "This Cream is burned too—why Madam, the bishop has set his foot in it." As late as 1875, the phrase appeared in another text: "Th' milk's bishopped again!" In any case, the connection linking church officials, heretics, and burned food supposedly inspired the modern exclamation "Now you've put your foot in it!," applied to any botched situation, whether in the kitchen or out of it.

[3] Similarly, the French culinary term *cardinaliser* means "to plunge crustaceans into boiling liquid," thus turning them the color of the church official's garments. The recipe for *pears cardinal* calls for poaching the fruits in vanilla syrup, then topping them with kirsch-flavored raspberry sauce and almonds. A cardinal's crimson clerical robes also inspired the name of the red mullet known as *cardinal*—and, for that matter, that of the North American bird of the same name.

have been credited with inventing the popular mix of espresso and steamed milk. This monastic order, incidentally, takes its name from the Italian word *cappuccio,* or "hood"—a word that also inspired the French and Italian names for the edible flower known in English as the *nasturtium.* Known in France as a *capuchine* and in Italy as a *cappuccina,* the nasturtium plant bears brilliant orange and yellow blossoms, part of which resemble a little pointed hood.

The decidedly humble attire of monks also inspired the name of the French dessert *quatre mendiants* (in English, *four mendicants*), a dish of figs, raisins, nuts, and almonds, whose colors recall those worn by the four mendicant, or "begging," orders, the Franciscans, the Dominicans, the Carmelites, and the Augustinian Hermits. (The *mendicant,* or "begging," in their name, by the way, comes from the Latin *mendum,* meaning "fault" or "physical defect," and is a relative of the English *mend* and *amend.*)

The seafood-menu entrée *monkfish* is also a nod to pious types. Etymologists suspect that this sea creature's unusually heavy and oddly shaped head reminded some observers of a fish wearing a monk's cowl. A more comical image of a friar rears its head in the name *tête de moine,* or *monk's head,* a name for Bellelay, a cheese that not only resembles a tonsured pate but originated in a monastery in Bellelay. Then there's the thin pan fritter known in Spain as *orejas de abad* and in Portugal as *orelhas-de-abade,* both of which translate as "abbot's ears."

Ironically, the spectacularly rich and elegant Parisian dessert called a *religieuse* commemorates one who has taken a vow of poverty—namely, a "nun." A pyramid of éclairs filled with coffee, chocolate, or vanilla-flavored cream, the base of a *religieuse* is iced with dark chocolate so that it resembles a nun's habit, followed by cream-colored piping for a "collar," and topped with a "head" of lighter-colored chocolate.

Our forebears seem to have taken a special delight in applying naughty "nun" names to several other foods. Among the delights of Portuguese cuisine, for example, is a sweet egg pudding known as *barriga de freira,* or "nun's tummy," the reason apparently being that eating too many of these calorific confections will leave a person "fat as a nun" (or some nuns, anyway). In southern Italy, pastry-shop shelves hold *zinne di monaca,* or "nun's tits"—round Neapolitan cakes topped with icing and a candied cherry. And bite into a plum that some Italians call a *coscia delle monaca,* and you've bitten a "nun's thigh."

The temptation to snicker about what might be going on under a nun's robes is even more widespread, judging by the number of dishes with names that translate as "nun's farts." In southern Germany, fried homemade noodles that are tossed into soups or served with powdered sugar and coffee go by the dialectal (and perhaps onomatopoetic) name *Nonnafuerzla.* In parts of France and Switzerland, "nun's farts," or *pets de nonne,* are walnut-sized fritters that are (noisily) deep-fried and then sprinkled with fine sugar. For the easily embarrassed, this name is sometimes euphemized as *soupirs de nonne*, or "nun's sighs." In parts of South America, a type of fried yeast cake is called *suspiro de monja*, which also translates as "nun's sighs," although sometimes they go by the naughtier name *bolas de fraile*, or "friar's balls" or "monk's balls." (When prudish New Englanders needed a word for a similar fritter, however, they chose the more respectable *Baptist cake*, so named because it's dipped in hot oil, much as Baptist believers are dipped in water. This practice is reflected in the denomination's name, which derives from the Greek *baptein*, "to dip.")

Noisy nuns are also immortalized by the kind of fried cakes known in parts of Italy as *chiacchiere delle suore*. Popular during Carnivale, these cakes go by a name that means "nun's chatter," alluding to the sound they make while frying.

The Pope endures his own share of tweaking from fanciful food names. In English, the fatty rectal bump on a fowl is jocularly known as the *pope's nose*. (This tidbit is the subject of contention in an early scene in James Joyce's *Portrait of the Artist as a Young Man*.) The likening of this nose-shaped protuberance to the pope's proboscis is thought to have come about as a culinary dig at Catholics during the reign of England's James II. At any rate, this part of a fowl sometimes goes by the name *parson's nose*. In Spain, it's *el obispillo*, or "the little bishop."[4]

---

[4] In France, this morsel goes by the delightful name *le sot-l'y-laisse*, which translates as something like "only silly people won't eat it"—or literally, "the silly person leaves it where it is."

Pope's eye is a name for the lymphatic gland from the middle of a leg of mutton, regarded by epicures as a delicacy. (The great eighteenth-century lexicographer Samuel Johnson defined the term *pope's eye* succinctly and shruggingly: "The gland surrounded by fat in the middle of the thigh: why so called I know not.") In Germany, the *pope's eye* is called a *Pfaffensbisschen,* or "priest's bit," the implication being that this choice piece should be reserved for a priest. In France, the gland also has a religious connection, but one that's more sinister: The French call this morsel the *œil de Judas,* or "eye of Judas," a reference to the disciple who betrayed Jesus.

Speaking of the pope, a papal summer vacation spot happens to have inspired the name of a familiar fruit: Long ago, popes escaped from the pressures of being pope at a vacation villa outside Rome at *Cantalupo.* It was here that the Italians first cultivated a delicately flavored fruit from Armenia. The memory of this papal getaway remains inside the name of that sweet muskmelon also known as the *cantaloupe.*

Linguistic relics of various saints are preserved in several food names. The appellation *Saint Peter's fish* applies to several different denizens of the deep, all of which are distinguished by having a spot on either side of their bodies. Appearing on French menus as *Saint-Pierre* and Italian ones as *San Pietro,* this is the fish traditionally thought to be mentioned in a passage from Matthew 17:27, where Jesus offers financial advice to Peter after the disciple worries about how he's going to find the money to pay his taxes that year: "[G]o to the sea and cast a hook, and take the first fish that comes up, and when you open its mouth you will find a shekel; take that and give it to them for me and for yourself." Legend has it that the marks on the side of *Saint Peter's fish* were made by the obedient apostle's thumb and forefinger while he retrieved the coin from its mouth. This name now applies to such fish as the haddock and the John Dory.[5] *Saint Peter's ear*, meanwhile, is an edible, pointy-shelled Mediterranean mollusk, the name of which recalls the moment when the apostle Peter grabbed his sword and sliced off the ear of one of those who came to arrest Jesus.

Scallops broiled in a creamy wine sauce and topped with bread crumbs or cheese are called *coquilles Saint-Jacques*, after the impetuous fisherman turned apostle James (*Jacques*, in French). Tradition holds that this martyred saint's remains were entombed at the shrine of Santiago de Compostela, a Spanish town famous as

---

[5] The golden-yellow fish called a *John Dory*, incidentally, was for centuries called simply a *dory*, from the French *doré*, or "gilded," a descendant of the Latin *deaurāre*, "to gild." This makes the fish's name an etymological relative of such words as *aureole*, literally, "halo," and the elemental notation *Au*, meaning "gold." Another of these "golden" words is the French cooking term *dorure*, or "gilding," which is made by brushing thinned egg yolks onto pastry. The *John* in the *John Dory*'s name was added in the 1700s, apparently due to the influence of a popular song about a French pirate by that name.

a shrine for the medieval faithful, which adopted the scallop shell as its symbol.

The breast-shaped Italian cookies *minni ∂i'Sant' Agata,* or "Saint Agatha's nipples," recall the grisly tale of Agatha, a Sicilian who suffered sexual harassment at the hands of a government official. When she resisted his advances, the official threatened to expose her as a Christian, at a time when such believers were harshly persecuted. When that threat failed as well, he sent her off to a house of ill repute, hoping to corrupt her. Even there, however, Agatha remained steadfastly chaste.

Unfortunately, things went from bad to worse, and Agatha prayerfully endured a series of tortures, the most famous of which was the slicing off of her breasts. Throughout Western art Saint Agatha is depicted holding a platter bearing her severed breasts, *à la* Salome with the head of John the Baptist. Bloodied but unlaid, Agatha finally departed this earth after being rolled in hot coals, and for her efforts she was declared a saint.

Another sweet but morbid mouthful is the Spanish candy traditionally served on All Saints' Day, *huesos ∂e santo,* or "saint's bones." These tubes of marzipan paste are stuffed with an egg-and-sugar mixture or sweet fillings made of truffles or fruit.[6]

---

[6] The *huesos,* or "bones," in *huesos ∂e santo,* incidentally, belong to a bony linguistic family that includes such English words as the "porous bone" condition known as *osteoporosis.* The Spanish *hueso* is also buried inside

The bean that yields the chocolate substitute *carob* sometimes goes by the name *locust bean* or *Saint John's bread*. This name arose out of confusion about the English translations of passages in the gospels of Matthew and Mark, which note that while living in the wilderness John the Baptist subsisted on "locusts and wild honey." While some believe this meant that the prophet made meals of swarming insects, others have assumed that instead he was eating the more appetizing carob bean also known as a *locust*. (*Carob*? Its etymology is far less exciting: It comes from the Arabic *kharrūbah*, which means "bean pod" or simply "carob.")

That beloved French pastry the *Saint-Honoré* honors the patron saint of pastry cooks and bakers. (However, according to the *Larousse Gastronomique*, accounts of this seventh-century bishop's life are completely unclear as to why he should be associated with matters gastronomic.)

Because the late-August feast day of Saint Philibert coincides with the yearly ripening of hazelnuts, this seventh-century French abbot's name apparently inspired a word that also means "hazelnut," *filbert*. (These dainty little nuts, in turn, inspired the English expression *filbert nails*. In the eighteenth century, *filbert nails* meant "perfectly formed fingernails." Anthony Trollope once de-

the name of the island at the southernmost tip of Florida known to Spanish explorers as *Cayo Hueso*, or "Bone Island." The Spanish *cayo* means "small island," and the term *Cayo Hueso* itself was adapted by English speakers into a name that seemed more familiar and inviting (and logical, considering its location), *Key West*.

scribed someone with "clear white hands, filbert nails."
Trollope's contemporary Richard H. Barham sang the
praises of a "pretty little hand" with "filbert-formed
nails." For unknown reasons, *filbert* also now denotes
someone who, according to *Webster's Third New International Dictionary,* "presumes to be an expert analyst,"
such as a *football filbert.*)

Several other food names suggest a sort of love-hate
relationship with certain clergy. Those irregular,
twisted strings of Italian pasta known as *strozzapreti* go
by a name that literally translates as "strangle-priests."
Sort of along the same lines, the fiery Brazilian chili
pepper called *mata-frade* has a name that means "it kills
the friar." A heart-shaped confection baked at convents
and monasteries in certain parts of Spain goes by the
creepy name *corazón de obispo,* or "bishop's heart."

Other food names seem to reflect a certain delight in
the notion that pious folk may slip up and succumb to
worldly inducements just like the rest of us. In this
country, there's *tipsy parson,* a type of sherry-soaked,
almond-topped sponge cake once popular in the South.
In Austria, one popular liquor-soaked cake is called a
besoffener Kapuziner, or "drunk monk," specifically a
Capuchin. Another example is *Jansson's Temptation,* a
hearty recipe of potatoes, onions, anchovies or herring,
and cream. This dish is named after Swedish religious
reformer Erik Jansson, who in 1846 fled to this country with a group of followers, preached a gospel of
strict asceticism, and urged converts to adopt the most
meager of diets. According to *Food & Wine* magazine,

51

legend has it that "an ardent follower discovered Jansson surreptitiously devouring a steaming casserole of potatoes and anchovies enriched with milk, onions, and butter. He was gorging so passionately that his reputation was forever ruined, and the dish was thereafter called *Jansson's Temptation.*"

Speaking of yielding to temptation, in Puritan New England, spices such as fennel and dill were sometimes called *meeting seeds.* The reason, according to John F. Mariani's *Dictionary of American Food and Drink,* was that these seeds were often chewed during Sunday church meetings, "probably to mask the smell of alcohol on one's breath." And speaking of religious hypocrisy, the name of the large, covered French cooking pot called a *marmite* supposedly derives from an Old French word for "hypocrite" because the lid makes it impossible to see what's really going on inside.

Bishop's bread, a sweetened bread filled with dried fruit, supposedly is so named because a resourceful Kentucky homemaker improvised a recipe for such a loaf when her local clergyman dropped by unexpectedly for a visit. However, this story has the ring of folk etymology, particularly since a similar bread called *Bischofbrot* has been popular in Germany for centuries. (Incidentally, the idea of hospitality toward drop-in clergy also figures in the use of the English phrase *like the curate's egg,* which alludes to "a carefully chosen diplomatic response." According to a well-worn story, this expression originated when a parishioner served a badly cooked scrambled egg to a visiting curate, then asked the clergyman's opinion. Gingerly wiping his mouth, the circumspect minister hesitated, then charitably replied, "Parts of it are excellent.")

Then there's the succulent eggplant dish that goes by the Turkish name *imam bayildi,* which translates as "the priest fainted." Tradition holds that it was once served to an imam who found its mere fragrance so heavenly that he passed out with pleasure. (Another story goes that the imam gave his daughter an expensive jar of olive oil as a wedding present and she used it up in just a few days making this dish, which caused her father to faint. Whatever the story, a similar idea apparently inspired the Welsh dish called *swooning priest,* which prominently features an ingredient named for the town in Wales that first produced it, *Caerphilly cheese.*)

One more clergyman lives on in a common food name: the Reverend Sylvester Graham, an eccentric Presbyterian minister from Connecticut who promoted a strict, abstemious diet that won him countless converts during America's health craze of the 1820s and 1830s. Convinced that eating meat and fat leads to sinful sexual excess, the good reverend urged total vegetarianism. He also warned that mustard and ketchup cause insanity, urged followers to drink only water, and recommended sleeping with one's windows open regardless of the weather. More reasonably, he touted the merits of a high-fiber diet and promoted the use of homemade unsifted wheat flour instead of refined white flour. Inspired by his example—and knowing a market niche and a marketable name when they saw one—bakers created a line of whole-wheat snacks they called *Graham crackers.*

Among Graham's most ardent followers was Dr. James Caleb Jackson, one of the first nineteenth-century physicians to advocate replacing the traditional breakfast of hot gruel with a vitamin-enriched cold cereal. According to *Panati's Extraordinary Origins of Everyday Things,* Dr. Jackson developed his own branny breakfast cereal and, combining the name of his hero with the word *bran,* called his high-fiber creation *Granula.* It was only later, in the 1890s, that health faddist Dr. John Kellogg, who regularly downed seven graham crackers for breakfast, came up with his own cereal, which he called *Granola*—a proprietary name which, like Kleenex, Xerox, and many other others, has long since become a generic term, at least in the public mind.

Religious affiliation—or nonaffiliation—occasionally figures in food names, such as the Cuban dish of black beans and rice that, because of its appearance, is called *moros y cristianos,* literally, "Moors and Christians." (The word *Moor,* by the way, may be linked to the Greek word *mauros,* meaning "dark," or "black," a word thought to be related to the name of the dark, bitter cherry called a *morello* as well as to that of the delectable, dark-capped mushroom known as a *morel.*) A less tolerant attitude toward differing religious beliefs appears in an old German word for "buckwheat": because this grain was introduced to Europe in the fourteenth century from the unchristianized Middle East, it was known as *Heidenkraut,* literally, "heathen plant."

Hot Cross Buns and Halibuts

Some familiar food names contain surprising images of Christian iconography. Although the *passion fruit* certainly sounds as if it is a powerful aphrodisiac, its name actually recalls Christian symbols commemorating the torture and crucifixion of Jesus. In its earliest sense, the English word *passion* meant "suffering," deriving from the Latin stem *pass-*, meaning "to suffer." From this root also originated the word for someone who suffers ill health, a *patient*, and our term for the sense of "suffering with" someone, *compassion* — and eventually *passion* came to denote more generalized "powerful feelings" involving sex, love, joy, or anger.

The passion fruit, in any case, is named for the *passion flower* plant that bears it, whose blossom is so complicated it looks as if it had been put together by a committee. Spanish conquistadors who happened upon this spectacularly odd-looking flower in the Americas projected onto it their own religious symbolism for the passion and crucifixion of Jesus: In its tendrils, they saw whips. In its showy filaments, they saw the crown of thorns. They compared its leaves to spears, its stamens to hammers, its ten sepals to the faithful apostles present at the crucifixion, and other parts to nails, flesh wounds, and a halo.

The "tears of Christ," on the other hand, are memorialized in a strong, sweet red wine from southern Italy now widely known by its medieval Latin name, *Lachryma Christi.* In parts of France, wine and the young Jesus are linked in a pair of still more picturesque, if sacrilegious, phrases: if a white wine is particularly exquisite, it's said colloquially that *"C'est comme si le petit Jésus faisait pipi dans ma bouche,"* or "It's as if little Jesus peed in my mouth." Of a particularly rich red wine, the French say, *"C'est le petit Jésus en coulotte de velours,"* or "It's little Jesus in velvet breeches." (A similarly irreverent compliment paid to fine French wine: *"C'est du pipi d'ange,"* or roughly, "It's like an angel's piss.")

Jesus' mother, on the other hand, inspired the name of the sweet German libation *Liebfraumilch,* or "Milk of the Blessed Mother," which originated in the vineyards of a church by the same name. There have been other linguistic sightings of the Blessed Virgin in kitchens as well. Many scholars suspect that her name is embedded in that of the cooking method called *bain-marie,* or "Mary's bath." This technique, in which a dish is heated by placing it in a pan of warm water, is apparently named for its exceeding gentleness.

A faint trace of Christian imagery is visible within the name of that decorative candy called *marzipan,* also known as *marchpane,* made of crushed almonds or almond paste, egg whites, and sugar or honey, which is then molded into shapes such as fruits or animals. The origins of the word *marzipan* stretch back to the Italian word *marzapane,* which for a time meant "little box for candies" but earlier still referred to a "small container for rare coins." This word for "coin box," in turn, is thought to derive ultimately from the Arabic *mawtabān,* or "king sitting still," a derisive name given by the Saracens to a type of Venetian coin stamped with the figure of Jesus seated on a throne. The etymological history of this traditional Easter treat was further confused due to another food term in Medieval Latin, *Marco pānis,* or "Mark's bread," which denoted another festive treat also served in April on the feast day of Saint Mark.

In fact, the events of the weeks leading up to Easter, the climactic date on the Christian calendar, have inspired the names of many festive foods, such as the brioche-style *King cake.* Often topped with purple, green, and gold icing, it's wildly popular during the Louisiana carnival season. Traditionally, every *King cake* contains a red bean, sometimes covered in gold or silver leaf, although in the past imaginative bakers have replaced the bean with everything from a piece of gold to diamonds, peas, beans, pecans, coins, and tiny baby Jesus dolls. Whatever the hidden treasure, the person who happens upon it can expect good luck.

The English word *carnival* is another food word of sorts, one that derives from the Latin for "a lifting or removal of meat." Originally, *carnival* specified the evening of the first day of Lent (also known as Ash Wednesday), which commenced the forty days during which the faithful were supposed to abstain from eating meat. This final blowout came to be known as *Mardi Gras,* literally "Fat Tuesday." As time went on, the word *carnival* came to refer to a whole season of wintertime revelry and later was extended still further to more general types of festivities. The word *carnival* belongs to a fleshy linguistic family that includes *carnal, carnage, carnivore,* and *chili con carne.*[7] The *levare,* or "lifting," inside *carnival* makes it a relative of such lightweight words as *leaven, levity, relieve, alleviate,* and *legerdemain,* or "lightness of hand," as well as the adjective describing something that doesn't weigh much, *light.*

The deep-fried potato pastries known in English as *fastnachts* or *fasnachts* are another example of a food whose name derives from a specific period on the Christian calendar. They take their name from German *Fastnacht,* or "Shrove Tuesday," and originated in the day-before-Lent practice of using up all the animal fat that was soon to be forbidden. Carnivores who give up eating animal flesh during this time may decide to supplement their diets with small round breads that bear a cross made of frosting, the traditional Lenten favorites known as *hot cross buns.* Although the frosted *X* marks them as Christian, the tradition of baking small cakes to celebrate spring and the advent of new life actually harks back to much earlier pagan times.

Another familiar food name deriving from an association with religious holidays is *halibut.* In the thirteenth

---

[7] It's also kin to *carnation,* which can refer either to those parts of a painting that depict bare flesh—as in "This artist's carnation is excellent"—or to the flower that some etymologists think is named for the color of Caucasian skin. (Others, however, suspect that the *carnation*'s name evokes not simply "flesh" but "bleeding flesh," an allusion to the deep red color of some varieties of this blossom.)

century, the word *butt* had many of the same meanings it has today. Among them was the sense of *butt* meaning "flatfish," such as sole, fluke, and turbot. The largest of these flatfishes, the *halibut*, which can grow to weigh as much as seven hundred pounds, has a name that was formed by adding *butt* to the Middle English *hali*, or "holy," because it was eaten on holy days. Similarly, although the etymology of *turbot* isn't entirely clear, the name of this brown fish with a distinctively knobby surface is thought to be related to the Old Swedish *törnbut*, *törn* meaning "thorn," and *but* meaning "flatfish."

Gods, Goddesses, and Other Supernatural Foods

Ghostly outlines of other gods and mythical figures also haunt the kitchen. From the name of the Roman goddess *Ceres*, who presided over agriculture and grain crops in particular, comes the name of that grainy fare *cereal*. The name *Ceres* itself stems from a linguistic root meaning "to grow," making it an etymological relative of such words as *increase*, *crescendo*, *create*, and *accrue*. The goddess's name also flavors the Spanish word for the grain-based beverage known as *cerveza*, or "beer," as well as *cerveza*'s Irish and Welsh cognates, *cuirm* and *cwrw*, the latter of which is pronounced "koo-roo."[8]

---

[8] *Green Goddess dressing*, however, has nothing to do with agricultural goddesses. This mixture of mayonnaise, anchovies, tarragon vinegar, pars-

Meanwhile, that gleeful hedonist and Roman god of wine, Bacchus, inspired the French expression *éperons bachiques,* literally "spurs of Bacchus," a general term applied to bite-size, cold hors d'oeuvres. Several foods celebrate the charms of Venus, the Roman goddess of erotic love, including the Italian pasta dish *umbilichi sacri,* or "sacred navels," another name for tortellini which are supposedly modeled after the goddess's belly button. The Italians sometimes apply the name *tete di Venere,* or "breasts of Venus," to those cherry-topped Italian pastries otherwise known as *zinne di monaca,* or "nun's breasts." French gets even more specific, applying the name *téton de Vénus,* or "nipple of Venus," to a kind of French peach—the *téton* being an etymological relative of *Grand Teton,* the highest mountain in the Teton range in Wyoming. (However, the French name for another variety of this suggestive fruit is *bonchrétien,* or "good Christian.")

According to Greek myth, the mint plant originally was a comely nymph named *Minthe,* who became the object of a spat between the god of the underworld, Pluto, and his kidnapped wife, Persephone. Depending on who's telling the story, either a jealous Persephone transformed Minthe into a fragrant herb to stop her from having an affair with her husband, or Pluto

ley, scallions, garlic, and other spices was created at San Francisco's Palace Hotel in the 1920s for actor George Arliss, who stayed there while performing in *The Green Goddess,* a play that later became one of the earliest "talkie" movies.

himself transformed the sweet young thing to protect her from Persephone's wrath.

Because his name automatically connotes great size, the king of the Roman gods, Jupiter, has his fingers in the names of a couple of food terms as well. Broccoli, for example, was once jocularly referred to as *the five green fingers of Jupiter.* The walnut used to be called *Jupiter's nut* because it belongs to the scientific genus *Juglans,* from Latin *Jovis glans,* or "Jove's acorn." The *-glans* in this name is cognate with those nut-shaped anatomical structures called *glands,* as well as the similarly shaped body parts known in medical terminology as the *glans penis* and the *glans clitoridis.* The ancient Greeks and Romans in fact considered walnuts fertility symbols and traditionally served them at weddings in the hope of ensuring that the couple produced many children.

Some foods are inextricably linked in the human mind not just with immortals but with immortality itself. The pudding *tansy,* which is made with the tart juice of the tansy plant, takes its name from the Greek word *athanasia,* or "immortality." According to the sixteenth-century English herbalist John Gerard, this is because the tansy's flowers "do not speedily wither." Both the plant and the pudding are etymological cousins of such words as *euthanasia,* or "good death," and *thanatopsis,* or "meditation on death," as well as *thanatophobia,* or "fear of death." With typically deathless prose, diarist Samuel Pepys dutifully recorded eating such a pudding one April day in 1666: "And there spent an houre or two with pleasure with her, and eat a tansy." In the Christian tradition, tansy was a regular feature at Easter meals, symbolizing the "bitter herbs" eaten on Passover. "Mince-pie," an eighteenth-century writer noted, "is as essential to Christmas, as . . . tansy to Easter." Even today in tony restaurants a sprig of curled tansy occasionally serves as a garnish.

For their part, Greek and Roman gods ensured their own immortality by dining on *ambrosia*, a name later given to a dessert of oranges and coconut flakes. The Greek word *ambrosia*, which was borrowed whole into English, comes from the Greek stems *a-*, meaning "not," and *-mbrotos*, or "mortal," making this food name a relative of several other words involving *mortality*, including *mortify, mortuary, moribund, rigor mortis*, and *murder. Ambrosia* is also a cousin of the Sanskrit name of the drink that enabled the Hindu gods to live forever, *amrita*.

Along with their ambrosia, the ancient Greek gods liked to sip the death-defying drink they called *nektar*, or, in Latin, *nectar*. This liquid's name comes from Greek words that mean "overcoming death." Thus the *nec* in *nectar* is related to such "deadly" or "damaging" words as *necrophilia, pernicious*, and *nocuous*, the last of these meaning "harmful," as opposed to *innocuous* or *innocent*. Nowadays the word *nectar* also refers to various sweet liquids, including the plant juice that bees sip (and, incidentally, later vomit) in order to make honey. The legendary sweetness of nectar also inspired the name of the aromatic fruit the *nectarine*.

If the thought of food that confers immortality sounds tantalizing, perhaps it's worth noting that the word *tantalize* itself commemorates a legendary king named Tantalus who ran into a little problem with food. In Greek myth, good King Tantalus infuriated the immortals by stealing their nectar and ambrosia to feed to mere humans. As punishment, the gods sentenced him to spend eternity in a pool of water that receded when he reached down to drink from it, and beneath clusters of luscious fruit that shrank from reach whenever he tried to pluck them.

One last divinely inspired food: chocolate. Although its name comes from the Aztecs' word *xocolātl*—literally, "bitter water"—the scientific name of the cocoa plant that produces it seems far more appropriate. The source of cocoa and chocolate is the tropical tree called *Theobroma*. A linguistic relative of such divine words as *theology, polytheism,* and *pantheon,* the scientific name *theobroma* literally means "food of the gods," as chocolate lovers everywhere will confirm.

3

MISHAPS
AND
HAPPY ACCIDENTS

Foods Named by Mistake

*M*angled translations, misunderstandings, geographical mix-ups, and other happy accidents have provided the English language with some of its most common and colorful terms for food and drink. Foods such as *peas, lemon sole, oranges, German chocolate cake, turkey, cherries, Jordan almonds,* and *refried beans* all owe their names to linguistic goofs of one sort or another. A close look at these felicitous foul-ups can help illuminate the way language sometimes works. In this chapter, we'll explore how such names come about, often as the result of that typically human impulse to take something seemingly foreign and turn it into something more familiar.

In addition, linguistic mishaps occasionally produce English terms that seem to have something to do with food but in fact do not. *Apple-pie order, to egg on, chowderhead, big cheese,* and *pea jacket* are just a few examples. We'll meet these and many more at the end of this chapter.

Words Misheard or Mistranslated

Consider the *cherry.* The Normans who conquered England called this fruit a *cherise,* a forerunner of the modern French *cerise.* The natives of the British Isles, however, mistakenly assumed that *cherise* was a plural and began referring to a single one of these fruits as a *cheri.* Several English words, in fact, were formed by a process known to linguists as *back-formation,* one type of which occurs when a singular word is mistakenly assumed to be a plural. (Another example is *kudos.* Many people assume that this word meaning "praise" or "acclaim" is a plural noun and speak of giving someone a *kudo.* Actually, there's no such thing as a single kudo, for the word *kudos,* an ancient Greek term for "glory," was borrowed whole into English.)

Another food word formed this way is *pea*, a descendant of the Middle English name of this legume, *pease*, as in the singsong nursery rhyme that begins "Pease porridge hot." By the early seventeenth century, the English began referring to a single one of these as a pea, although as late as 1614 Sir Walter Raleigh described something as being "of the bigness of a great Peaze." Both *pea* and *pease*, at any rate, are linguistic descendants of the ancient Greeks' word for "pea," *pison*.[1]

The same thing happened with *capers*. Among the ancient Greeks, the word *kapparis* denoted a shrub with flower buds that could be pickled and added to salads and fish dishes. The Romans adapted this name into *capparis*, which eventually found its way into Middle English as *caperis* or *capres*. Once again, speakers of modern English lopped off that final *s*, so that now one of these piquant buds is referred to as a *caper*.

The opposite may have happened with the *gherkin*. This small pickling cucumber's name apparently stems from a Middle Persian word for "watermelon," *angārah*, a term the Greeks later changed to *agouros* and applied

---

[1] Peas seem to have suffered from other misunderstandings as well. They were once considered a "low" and "unfit" food—an attitude articulated by a late-seventeenth-century English writer who sniffed, "It is a frightful thing to see persons so sensual as to purchase and eat green peas."

to watermelons as well as cucumbers. In Dutch, *agouros* became *gurk,* the plural of which is *gurken.*[2]

Similarly, many etymologists suspect that the word *muffin* arose, as it were, from the Low German *Muffen,* the plural form of *Muffe,* or "small cake." (True to its Germanic roots, by the way, the English language once formed plurals the same way as Dutch and German, by adding an *-en* to a singular noun. Vestiges of this practice are still visible in our words *oxen* and *children.*)

Several other foods got their names when strange-sounding parts of foreign words were changed to something that sounded more familiar. The *crayfish* or *crawfish,* for example, isn't a fish at all. Actually, this staple of Cajun cuisine has a name adapted from the Old French *crevice,* or "edible crustacean." *Crayfish* and *crevice* are linguistic cousins of the English *crawl* and *crab* and are unrelated to the English *crevice,* or "deep cleft," which comes from an entirely different root. At any rate, the Old French *crevice* skittered into Middle English as *crevise,* the tail end of which eventually evolved into the more recognizable *-fish.*

Another southern favorite, *hoppin' john,* apparently has nothing to do with either hopping or anyone named John. Some lexicographers believe this traditional

---

[2] Another Dutch plural now resides in English as part of the name of an island near Manhattan. This site, purchased by a Dutchman in 1630, was named for the Netherlands' governing body at the time, the *Staten Generaal,* or "States General." Today, of course, it's known as *Staten Island.*

New Year's Day stew of black-eyed peas, rice, and bacon or salt pork may take its name from a Caribbean dish called *pois à pigeon,* or "pigeon peas," an expression variously adapted into *hoppin' john* or *happy john.*[3]

A similar mangling of a French name occurred with the shortbread known as *petticoat tails.* This term dates from sixteenth-century Scotland, where the Francophilic courtiers of Mary Stuart called them *petits gâtels,* which later became *petits gâteaux,* or "little cakes." Somewhere along the way the Scots apparently decided that *petits gâteaux* sounded a lot like *petticoat tails* and started calling them that. They even began baking them in a ring pan with scalloped edges, so that now the cookies also bear a resemblance to their frilly namesake.

Jordan almonds, those large nuts covered with a smooth, hard candy coating in various pastel colors, come not from Jordan but from Spain. Their name actually derives from the Old French *jardin,* meaning "garden." This descriptive was adopted into Middle English, in which a fine variety of almond was called a *jardin almaund*—but English speakers soon anglicized it, despite the risk of geographical confusion.

Another food-related adaptation of a French word is the term *kickshaw,* which now means "a fancy food or

---

[3] Less credible explanations include one that links this stew with a New Year's Day ritual that requires children to hop around the table before sitting down to eat. At any rate, a similar dish of red beans and rice is known in parts of the South as *limpin' suzan,* probably formed by analogy.

delicacy." *Kickshaw* comes from the French *quelque chose*, meaning "something." In the past, the British used both *quelque chose* and *kickshaw* interchangeably and, somewhat contemptuously, to denote "a 'something' French"—that is, food prepared in an overly fancified, Frenchified way as opposed to more substantial English fare. Thus in 1655, a persnickety English writer dismissed what he called "over curious cookery, making... *quelque-choses* of unsavoury ... Meat."

Another French word misheard resulted in the name of the fish we call *lemon sole*. Actually, this fish is a type of flounder, not sole, and has nothing at all to do with the tart yellow fruit, even though it may be served with a thin slice of it. The name *lemon sole* derives instead from a French term for "flatfish," *limande*. It's thought that *limande*, in turn, may derive from the French word *lime*, meaning "file" or "rasp," because of this creature's rough outer layer. Another theory holds that the name *limande* (and, ultimately, *lemon sole*) comes from the Latin word for "mud," *līmus*, a reference to the bottom-dwelling habits of flatfish.[4] (If the latter is true, then the enticing lemon sole is a close linguistic relative of the less-than-enticing words *slime* and *limaceous*, or "sluglike.")

The word *cutlet* is another French derivative that isn't what it seems: it's not, as one might reasonably suppose,

---

[4] *Flounder* itself comes from a whole school of "flat" words, including *flat, plateau, plate, platitude* (literally, something "flat" or "lacking in originality"), and *plane.* The flat *flounder* is also related etymologically to the sweet and creamy "flat" dessert called *flan.*

a "little cut" of meat. Instead, *cutlet* comes from the French *côtelette,* a descendant of the Latin *costa,* or "rib." This makes *cutlet* an etymological relative of several other words involving "ribs," "flank," or "sides," including the large, "ribbed" English cooking apple known as a *costard,* as well as the tender *entrecôte* steak that's cut from "between the ribs." All of these words are also kin to *accost*—literally "to approach the side" of something or someone, not to mention the word designating the "rib" or "side" of a landmass, *coast.*

Similarly, *spareribs* aren't "extra" ribs. Rather, this is an English alteration of the Low German *ribbesper,* or "pork ribs roasted on a spit [or spear]," from Old German words for "rib" and "spear." (The same idea is still reflected in the modern German word for "spareribs," *Rippespeer*—literally, "spear ribs.") The English adopted the Old German word and altered it to *ribspare,* a term for "sparerib" that persists in England even today. More of them, however, switched the elements of this compound in a way that not only seemed to make more sense but was also reinforced by the fact that ribs tend to be closely trimmed of meat or, in other words, rather "spare."

The name of the savory spice *rosemary* is also misleading. Because this minty herb grew wild on the sea cliffs of southern Europe, the Romans called it *ros marīnus,* literally "sea dew." Thus the *ros-* in *rosemary* means "dew" and is related to the obsolete English words for "dewy," *roscid* and *rorid.* The *-mary* in *rosemary,* meanwhile, comes from a large pool of *marine* words, including *mermaid, maritime,* and *marinara.* (The last of these, referring to "sailor-style" sauce, apparently refers to the fact that the ingredients in marinara sauce were less likely to spoil at sea and could easily be prepared with a minimal use of fire—always a concern aboard wooden vessels).[5] English speakers who inherited the herb's name as *rōs marīnus* twisted it into the more familiar *rosemary,* a combination no doubt influenced by the traditional association between the Virgin Mary and her floral symbol, the rose.

For that matter, even *refried beans* aren't what they seem. Although their name seems like a reasonable translation of Spanish *frijoles refritos,* the fact is that these beans aren't really fried twice. In Spanish, *refritos* literally means "*well*-fried," not "*re*-fried."

(Speaking of beans, the name *fava bean* is a pleonasm—a redundancy, in other words, like the phrase "free gift." The Latin word *faba* means "broad bean," making a *fava bean* a "broad bean bean." *Azuki bean* is similarly redundant, given that *azuki* is a Japanese word deriving from the Chinese *xiǎo dòu,* literally, "small bean."[6] Equally redundant is the word *saltcellar,*

---

[5] All of these "marine" words are also related to the name of the sea cucumber, *bêche-de-mer,* a French adaptation of a Portuguese expression meaning "worm of the sea." The *bêche* in its name is a relative of the English *beast.* Also called a *trepang* (an adaptation of its Malaysian name), this sea creature is often dried or smoked and used to flavor Chinese soups.

[6] The *dòu* in *xiǎo dòu,* by the way, also appears in the Chinese expression *doufu,* meaning "fermented or curdled bean." It's the linguistic source of

which applies to a tabletop dish for dispensing salt. It's a compound of the Middle English words *salt* and *saler* — but the word *saler* itself is an old word for "salt-cellar," making a *saltcellar* literally a "salt saltcellar.")

Likewise, a *geoduck* isn't a fowl but a huge, odd-looking edible clam that burrows in the sands of the Pacific Northwest coast. A geoduck can weigh up to five pounds, and its distinctive "neck," or siphon, which stretches several feet in length, cannot be withdrawn into its shell. Even its name sounds strange, for *geoduck* is pronounced "gooey duck." This name may be related to a pair of Chinook terms meaning "neck" and "something attached to something else."

Speaking of ducks and mistaken identity, *Bombay duck* is a fish, not a fowl. In parts of India and Southeast Asia, this silver-beige denizen of the deep is salted and sun-dried, then fried or grilled and served as a crisp accompaniment to curries. Also known as *bombil* or *bummaloe,* Bombay duck is especially plentiful during monsoon season, when it preys on small fish forced to the surface of the water by turbulence. Its fanciful name apparently arose from the fact that this fish is therefore especially easy to catch at that time of year.

Which brings us to the pink sparkling wine from Germany whose original name was twisted into some-

the Japanese *tofu,* a word that, incidentally, appears in one of the livelier insults in a country famed for scrupulous politeness: "*Tofu no kado ni atama wo butsukete shinde shimae,*" which means "Hit your head on a corner of tofu and die."

thing entirely different. Most authorities believe that in its earliest form, this beverage was called *Kalte Ende,* which translates as "cold end"—probably referring to the fact that it should be sipped either at day's end or after a meal. Somewhere along the way, however, the *Ende* was corrupted to *Ente,* which means "duck," giving rise to this drink's English name, *Cold Duck.*

Still other culinary terms arrived in our mouths through the linguistic process known as "misdivision," in which one of two words that often appear next to each other (such as an indefinite article and a noun) absorbs a letter from the other. This happened, for example, with the English words *newt* (originally *an ewt,* the *ewt* being a variant of *eft,* which also denotes that cold-blooded amphibian). It also happened with *nickname,* which is a smoothing-out of *an eke-name,* the *eke* coming from an Old English word meaning "also." The reverse of this process, in which a noun's initial *n* attaches itself to an indefinite article, resulted in such words as *apron* (which in fourteenth- and fifteenth-century England was *a napron*), as well as *adder* (originally, *a naddre,* a relative of the modern Irish and Welsh words for "snake," *nathir* and *neider*) and *umpire* (from *a noumpere,* a Middle English borrowing of a French word literally meaning "nonpeer"—that is, someone who suppposedly can be impartial because he or she is "neither of the two people directly involved in a dispute").

One food name apparently arising from such an erroneous division is *orange,* the roots of which stretch all the way back to the Sanskrit *nārangah* and may be related to the Tamil word *naru*, or "fragrant." The initial *n* remains in the Spanish word for orange, *naranja*, as well as in its Romanian equivalent, *naranta*. The *n* dropped out of the Sanskrit word's Italian offspring, *narancia*, however, so that in modern Italy, this fruit is an *arancia*. The same occurred in French, where *une narange* gave way to *une orange*, an adaptation that led to the modern English name for the fruit. In addition, many etymologists theorize that the initial *o* in *orange* came about in part under the influence of the Old French word for "gold," *or*.

Something similar happened with *humble pie*. The *humble* in *humble pie* actually comes from an older English word, *numbles*, meaning the choicest edible innards or loins of an animal, usually deer. Over the years, *a numble pie* gave way to *an umble pie*, which isn't all that different, in terms of pronunciation, from *an humble pie*, especially for those not in the habit of pronouncing their *h*'s to begin with. Meanwhile, to those of more urbane tastes, the thought of eating numbles seemed increasingly humble—so much so that by 1665 Samuel Pepys grumbled about umbles in his famous diary, complaining that a recent host "did give us the meanest dinner, (of beef, shoulder and umbles of venison)." Nearly two hundred years later, American writer James Russell Lowell outlined the anti-umbles case even more firmly, observing, "Disguise it as you will, flavor it as you will, call it what you will, umble-pie is umble-pie, and nothing else." And today, the prospect of eating a plateful of the once-noble humble pie is even less appealing, no matter how you slice it.

Words Arising from Geographical Mix-ups

Some foods' names imply that they came from countries other than the ones where they actually originated. *German chocolate cake*, with its distinctive frosting of coconut and pecans, isn't so called because it's traditional German fare but because the original recipe, published in a Texas newspaper in 1957, called for *Baker's German's Sweet Chocolate*. But both the *Baker* and the *German* are misleading: *Baker's* refers not to the fact that the ingredient was a favorite among bakers but to the man who financed the first chocolate factory in the United States, Dr. James Baker. The *German's* refers to an employee of one of Dr. Baker's descendants, one Samuel German, who is credited with developing the sweet chocolate that would eventually bear his surname.

The pastry called a *Danish* probably isn't Danish at all. It appears to have originated in Austria—and indeed, the Danes refer to a Danish as a *wienerbrød*, which means "Vienna bread." Similarly, *Swiss steak* is hardly an Alpine specialty. This dish of beef baked with tomatoes, onions, peppers, and various spices may take its name from the English term *swissing*, or *swizzing*, a word of unknown origin that refers to the process of running cloth through pairs of rollers to smooth it. In fact, butchers use a similar process to tenderize cheaper cuts of meat, running them through rollers to create the grid pattern that inspired the name *cube steak*.

Swiss cheese, on the other hand, isn't always Swiss. Often it's just a holey American imitation of the world-famous cheeses known as *Emmenthaler* and *Gruyère*, both named for the valleys in which they're produced. And the strong cheese known as *Liederkranz* is named not for a German town but for a popular turn-of-the-century choral society in upstate New York whose members were particularly fond of this cheese. Its name literally means "wreath of song" and is a linguistic relative of the name that means "wreath of roses," *Rosenkranz*.

French fries probably aren't French, either. Many authorities believe they originated in Belgium in the nineteenth century and only later spread to France, where they're called *pommes frites*. The *French* in *French fry* actually derives from a cooking method called "frenching," which involves slicing vegetables into long thin strips, as in *French green beans* and *Frenched tenderloin*. Similarly, what Americans call *French dressing* has no counterpart in France, and *Russian dressing* isn't Russian. The latter got its name because the earliest versions of the mixture of mayonnaise, pimentos, chives, ketchup, and spices included a distinctly Russian ingredient: caviar.

And while *vichyssoise* may be an homage to the French spa town of *Vichy*, the first batch of this creamy potato-and-leek soup was actually whipped up in New York City early in the twentieth century. Indeed, much of so-called "classic" Italian cuisine —*fettucine primavera, veal parmigiana*, and *chicken Tetrazzini*, as well as *spaghetti and meatballs* —was created right here in the United States.

Then there's *turkey*, a fowl that is not native to the country of the same name. Indeed, this bird's American origins inspired Benjamin Franklin's famous proposal to make the turkey our national bird and place its likeness on the American flag. The eagle, he maintained, is "of bad moral character, like those among men who live by sharping and robbing," while the turkey is "a much more respectable bird and withal a true original native of America."

The name *turkey* was first applied to the African guinea fowl, which had been introduced to the British Isles by Turkish traders. Around the same time, Spanish conquistadors were bringing back turkeys from Mexico, and soon English speakers had hopelessly confused the gobbler and the guinea fowl. A similar confusion reaches across several languages. In modern French, a turkey is a *dindon*, a word that comes from an earlier name for it, *poulet d'Inde*, which literally means "hen of India" (in Russian, an *indeika*). Similarly, Germans once called the turkey a *Kalekuttisch Hün*, or "hen of Calcutta," although in modern Germany it is usually a *Truthahn* or *Truthenne*—a *Hahn* being male, a *Henne* being a "hen," and *trut* being the sound a German makes when trying to call either one of them.[7] Spaniards who encountered

---

[7] Incidentally, in Scotland a *bubbly-jock* isn't a giddy or overly enthusiastic athlete but a dialectal term for "turkey."

this unfamiliar bird in the Americas applied their name for "peacock," *pavo*, and in modern Spain, a turkey is a *pavo* and a peacock is a *pavo real*, or "royal peacock."

From the Latin *pāvō*, or "peacock," by the way, also comes the English word *pavonine*, or "peacocklike," and the direct borrowing from Italian, *pavonazzo*, "peacock-colored," usually applied to a type of dark reddish or purple marble. A version of *pāvō* also wound up in English as *poo*, an obsolete word that also means "peacock." *Poo* appears, in fact, in the 1382 Wyclif translation of the Bible, in a passage from II Chronicles listing a ship's cargo, of "gold, and syluer, and yuer, and apis, and poos." Modern translations more often render this as "gold, silver, ivory, apes, and peacocks."

Talking turkey, by the way, originally meant "saying pleasant things" or "talking agreeably." But later these turkey terms took on the meaning of "speaking frankly," "talking tough," "getting down to business," and finally *talking cold turkey*, as London's *Daily Express* explained in 1928: "She talked cold turkey about sex. 'Cold turkey' means plain truth in America." The connotation of clear-eyed, no-nonsense talk also seems to have influenced the term denoting a similarly stern treatment for addiction, *quitting cold turkey* — a phrase probably reinforced by the symptoms of drug withdrawal, including horripilation, or "goose-bumps," which make one's skin resemble a plucked turkey's.

Words That Intentionally Mislead

Like a last-minute addition of spice to make an unappealing dish more palatable, many food names apparently reflect a deliberate effort to cover up their true identities. *Welsh rabbit,* for example, is a meatless dish that can be as simple as melted cheese on toast or as complex as a sauce of cheese, butter, cayenne pepper, salt, and ale over buttered toast. The term for this cheap, filling meal has been around since at least the early eighteenth century. Another name for the same dish sounds even more exotic: *Welsh rarebit.* Similarly, *English monkey* is a mixture of bread crumbs, milk, butter, and cheese poured over crackers and garnished with tomatoes.

The plentiful supply of codfish off the northern Atlantic coast prompted New Englanders to apply the name *Cape Cod turkey* to their inexpensive meals of baked fish. And a century or two ago, New York's Hudson River so abounded with sturgeon that upstate dwellers called their exceedingly cheap fare *Albany beef.* (Sturgeon caviar was so plentiful that tavern owners regularly offered it as a free snack with drinks.)

Other food names sound even more wistful. American cowboys who endured countless meals of beans, beans, and more beans, jokingly tried to add a little linguistic seasoning to the monotony by christening them *Arizona strawberries, prairie strawberries,* or *Mexican strawberries.* Then there's *liberty cabbage,* a patriotic attempt during World War I to do away with the vegetable's

80

German name, *sauerkraut*. Like so many other attempts to reform everyday language by decree, the effort failed miserably.

And what discussion of food-name euphemisms would be complete without a mention of *Rocky Mountain oysters*? Testicles from a bull, lamb, or pig are also called *calf fries, prairie oysters, Spanish kidneys,* and simply *mountain oysters*. (According to Jane and Michael Stern, the intrepid authors of *Eat Your Way Across the USA,* these tidbits have inspired still more creative names, including *Jersey Jewels, Montana Tendergroin,* and, most picturesquely, *swinging beef*.) The organs, which can be fried, sautéed, braised, or poached, aren't on many Americans' Top Ten Appetizers list, even if they are considered a delicacy in France and Italy. (Perhaps this isn't surprising given this country's puritanical streak, which once prompted its more prudish citizens to substitute the phrases *a cow's father, a gentleman cow, a male cow, a Jonathan,* and simply *a cow creature* for the word *bull*.) The name *prairie oyster,* by the way, also applies to a cocktail made from an unbroken egg yolk, Worcestershire and Tabasco sauces, malt vinegar, salt, and pepper and traditionally offered by bartenders as a cure for hiccups. Then again, maybe merely eyeing a glass of such a mixture is enough to scare the hiccups out of anyone.

A few other foods have names that aren't intentionally misleading but are confusing nevertheless. An *egg cream,* that New York City favorite whose frothy head and rich consistency suggest it contains both eggs and cream, actually contains neither. First concocted around the turn of the century, when eggs were relatively expensive, an egg cream is made from chocolate syrup, ice-cold milk, and a jet of seltzer water. *Buttermilk*, likewise, contains no butter; it's simply the sour liquid that remains after the butterfat has been removed by churning.

Plum pudding is another misnomer. This dish usually contains bread crumbs, suet, raisins, currants and other fruits, eggs, spices, and sometimes brandy—in other words, just about everything but plums. As early as A.D. 725, our ancestors used the word *plum* or its variants to designate the familiar fleshy fruit, but from at least the seventeenth century, this word also denoted raisins or currants used in cooking, raisins being a good substitute if dried plums were unavailable. This interchangeable sense is clear in one late-eighteenth-century writer's wry observation that "Children, to whom you give a pill wrapped up in a raisin, will suck the plum and spit out the medicine." The spotted texture of plum pudding, in any case, inspired several terms, including *plum pudding mahogany*, a type of wood with a mottled finish, and *plum pudding dog*, a name that now applies, fittingly, to the pup otherwise known as a Dalmatian.

Finally, *Buffalo wings* exist nowhere in nature, of course. They're simply chicken wings, deep-fried and served with hot sauce and a blue-cheese dressing. They were invented in 1964 at the Anchor Bar in Buffalo, New York, by owner Teressa Bellissimo, who found herself simultaneously facing the problems of an oversupply of chicken wings and the need to come up with a snack for her son and his visiting friends. In 1977, according to *The Dictionary of American Food and Drink*, the city of Buffalo honored the accomplishment by proudly declaring July 29 "Chicken Wing Day."

Food Words That Aren't What They Seem

Just as gastronomic names sometimes fail to reflect a food's true origins or nature, many everyday words *seem* as though they have something to do with food, when in fact they do not. And often, these too are the results of mistranslations and misunderstandings.

There's nothing particularly orderly, for example, about a pie shell containing a jumble of sliced apples, sugar, and spices. But the expression *apple-pie order* denotes something that is "primly, properly in order." The reason may be that this sweet phrase is a corruption of French *nappes pliées*, which means "folded linen." Supporting this hypothesis is the fact that the old practice of "short-sheeting" a bed—folding its linens in half so that a would-be sleeper's legs won't fit into it—has long been known as making an *apple-pie bed*. (One nineteenth-century magazine writer described the results of such a practical joke: "He . . . began to fancy that the bed was too small for him, when . . . little Oxtowne . . . told him . . . 'it was only an apple-pie.'") Many lexicographers suspect the British borrowed the French phrase to describe such a bed, then transformed it into the more familiar-sounding *apple-pie bed* by the same type of misdivision that led to *humble pie* and *orange*. It certainly seems reasonable that, in a similar fashion, the phrase *nappes pliées* could give rise to *apple-pie order*, also suggesting the idea of efficiency as crisp and clean as neatly folded linens. (No word, however, on whether the practice of short-sheeting beds was also borrowed from the French—or if the British had been playing such practical jokes for years on their own.)

The term *big cheese*, meaning "an important person," does not refer to something from the dairy case but comes from the Persian and Urdu word *chīz*, which simply means "thing." Similarly, the expression *Cheese it!*, meaning "Look out!" or "Stop what you're doing and flee," may be simply an alteration of a similar imperative, "Cease it!," according to *Partridge's Concise Dictionary of Slang and Unconventional English*.

And while we're on the subject, it's worth noting that the term *green cheese* refers not to its color but to the fact that it's fresh and not yet thoroughly dried. The notion of the moon being made of such cheese apparently stems from an old expression suggesting that someone is so gullible that he or she would believe such a thing. Bishop John Wilkins mentioned such folk in 1638: "You may as soon perswade some Country Peasants, that the Moon is made of Green-Cheese (as we say) as that 'tis bigger than his Cart-Wheel." (Bishop Wilkins, incidentally, deserves a special place in the hearts of serious language lovers for his earnest efforts to develop a logical and universal language based on categories and subcategories—a page of which resembles a salmagundi of English, Arabic, Hindi, and modern-day computer emoticons. Unfortunately, his artificial language was so spectacularly complicated that it didn't get very far. Still, Wilkins's painstaking attempts to describe the pronunciation of various words continue to prove especially helpful to scholars attempting to reconstruct the sound of English in the years following the death of William Shakespeare.)

Many more words aren't what they seem. For example, even though chili peppers are a hot item these days, the word *chiliast* doesn't indicate someone who's fond of them, nor is a *chiliasm* the ecstatic result of biting into one. Actually, these are words we can expect to hear more of in the near future. A descendant of the Greek word *khilioi*, or "thousand," the word *chiliad* denotes both "a group containing a thousand elements" and the thousand years otherwise known as a "millennium." *Chiliasm* refers to the belief that Jesus will return to earth and reign for a thousand years. A *chiliast* is someone who believes in chiliasm. Similarly, a *chiliagon* refers to what must be a mind-boggling image—a geometric figure containing a thousand angles—while *chiliarchy* suggests the equally mind-boggling idea of "government by a thousand rulers."

Similarly, a *chowderhead* isn't a thick-soup enthusiast; it's someone who once might have been called a *jolterhead* or *jolthead*. These English slang terms, which are obscure in origin, apparently once referred to a large, thick, clumsy-looking head, then later came to refer less to the head's outer appearance than to its supposedly paltry contents. In 1605, Ben Jonson was apparently thinking of the earlier sense when he wrote, "Your red saucy cap, that seemes (to me) / Nayl'd to your iolthead." Some three and a quarter centuries later, F. Scott Fitzgerald used the latter sense when telling a correspondent, "I do not destinate to signify that you were a wiseacre, witling, dizzard, chowderhead." (Speaking of chowder and food words that aren't what they seem, the name *littleneck clams* doesn't refer to these creatures' anatomy. Originally, these small clams came from either Little Neck Bay on New York's Long Island or from Little Neck Bay, Ipswich, Massachusetts, although no one knows which for sure.)

Although the phrase *to egg on* may conjure up images of pelting people with eggs to nudge them into action, it has nothing to do with food. *Egg on* comes from the Old Norse *eggja,* "to incite"—a word closely related to the English *edge*—suggesting the image of nudging someone with the edge of a sword. In fact, *eggment* is an obsolete English word for "incitement" or "instigation." Chaucer used the word when repeating the patriarchal party line that "Thurgh wommannes eggement Mankynde was lorn [lost]." This type of *egging* belongs to a family of "pointed" words including *acme, acrid, acid,* and *eager* (the last of which used to mean "tart," "sharp," or "cutting"), as well as the name of the "wine turned 'sharp,'" *vinegar.* It's also related to *ear,* not the human or animal kind, which comes from a different linguistic source, but the sharp, spiky part of a cereal plant such as corn or wheat.

Likewise, a *pea jacket* isn't green, nor does any part of it resemble a pea. This heavy wool coat's name is probably an adaptation of the Dutch word for a type of jacket worn by sailors, *pijjekker*, from *pij*, a kind of coarse cloth, and *jekker*, or "jacket." From this Dutch word for a "coat of coarse woolen material" also comes the English name for a men's coat called a *pee*. Although this term is now unfortunately obsolete, it does appear in early English literature, such as the seventeenth-century text entitled *Love's Cure*, which includes the unintentionally memorable line "Your lashed shoulders [covered] with a velvet pee."

One of the most delicious words in the English language, the term *piepowder* has nothing to do with baking. It means "wayfarer," "traveler," "peddler," or "itinerant merchant." This word stems from the Medieval Latin *pede pulverosus*, literally "dusty-footed"—an apt description of a person who is often on the road. For centuries, the obsolete English word *dustyfoot* meant the same thing. The term *Court of Piepowders* denoted a kind of makeshift court assembled at medieval fairs and markets to settle grievances and administer justice among itinerant dealers and anyone else present who happened to be party to a dispute. In 1614, for example, the writer Ben Jonson described a fair "in whose Courts of Pye-pouldres I haue had the honour during the three dayes sometimes to sit as Iudge."

The *-powder* in *piepowder* belongs to a family of powdery words such as *pollen, pulverize,* and that trendy cornmeal mush *polenta. Piepowder*'s first syllable comes from a huge family of words having to do with feet— and, by extension, words involving the idea of "tripping up."[8] From the Germanic branch of this family, in which an initial *p* sound often changes to *f* in English, come the word *foot* and the name of the leg iron that goes just above it, *fetter.* From the Latin side come such terms as *pedal* and the sesquipedalian word *sesquipedalian,* which literally means "a foot and a half [long]" and refers to especially long and ponderous words or to someone who uses them a lot. This Latin "foot" source also gave us *impede,* "to put into fetters, hobble, shackle," and *expedite,* literally, "to free from a snare." The prehistoric source of all these "foot" words also produced the Latin word for "to sin," *peccāre*—literally, "to stumble"—leading to *impeccable,* or "not sinning" or "flawless," and, via Spanish, to the "little slip-up," "sin," or "fault" known as a *peccadillo.* Finally, another member of this "foot" family, Latin *impedicāre,* "to entangle" (from Latin *pedica,* "fetter"), gave rise to the Anglo-Norman *empecher,* "to impede or accuse." This in turn led to yet another member of this linguistic family that looks as if it might have something to do with food but doesn't: *impeach.*

Meanwhile, the term *small fry* has nothing to do with

---

[8] This "foot" connection is seen even more clearly in the French term for "piepowder," *pied poudreux.*

cooking but refers generally to the "offspring" or "progeny" of various kinds of animals, including fish. The etymology of *fry* in this sense is unclear, though it may be adapted from the Old Norse *freð* or *frae,* meaning "seed," a relative of the Gothic *fraiw,* meaning "seed" or "offspring." Therefore *salmon fry* refers not to a fish fry featuring this particular type of fish but to "the young of salmon." (Oddly enough, the notion of *fry* meaning "seed" led to the use of another wholly misleading term, the obsolete English word *egg-fry,* which actually means "spermatozoa.")

At least as early as 1577, English speakers began to extend the term *fry* to small humans, specifically to those deemed "insignificant beings." Thus, in 1689, Jonathan Swift would note charmingly, "As in a theatre the ignorant fry, / Because the cords escape their eye, / Wonder to see the motions fly." And in 1738, another writer would use the expression in relation to children, describing "A public School to teach all the young Fry of a Parish."

Finally, just as an ear of corn is the spiky, seed-bearing part on a stalk of that plant, a *wheatear* is the equivalent structure on a wheat stalk. But the word *wheatear* also applies not to a food but to a bird — namely, a small thrush with a gray back, buff-colored breast, and white tail. Because of this bird's pale back end, it was once called the *white arse.* In Cornwall, it still goes by the name *whiteass,* and elsewhere in England it's called a *white rump* or *wittol* ("white tail"). In the Netherlands and Germany, this little bird is a *witstaart* and a *Weiss-schwanz,* which also mean "white tail." And like *pea, cherry, caper,* and all those other food words stemming from misapprehended plurals, *wheatear* apparently was a back-formation from an alteration of *white arse,* namely *wheatears* — a word that likewise was misunderstood as a plural, so that a single one of them eventually came to be known as a *wheatear.*

Incidentally, the word *wheat* is an offshoot of a prehistoric root meaning "white," which makes wheat a linguistic relative of *white,* as well as *edelweiss* (the small and white, clean and bright flower whose name in German means "noble white") and *witloof,* another name for "endive," from the Middle Dutch words *wit* and *loof,* literally, "white leaf."

4

EDIBLE EPONYMS
AND
TASTY TOPONYMS

Foods Named for People and Places

*A*ncient military leaders and beloved opera stars, idle royalty and hardworking folk, ingenious chefs and savvy restaurateurs, actors, artists, composers, sailors, soldiers, government bureaucrats—all these have bequeathed their names to various foods. Linguists use the term *eponym* to refer to a person whose name inspires a whole new word. A nonfood example: *Mentor,* the ancient Greek character in the *Odyssey* who served as adviser to the son of Odysseus. From his name comes the English word *mentor.* (Similarly, from *Stentor,* the ancient Greek warrior whose voice, the *Iliad* tells us, "was as powerful as fifty voices of other men," comes our own word for a loud, deep voice: *stentorian.*)

Occasionally this process works in reverse, so that the name of a person or group of people derives from that of a food. As we'll see later in this chapter, these include the Roman orator Cicero and the Indian nation known as the Adirondack.

A place name that inspires a word is in turn called a *toponym.* Many fabrics get their names this way, such as *calico* (from Calicut, India), *paisley* (from Paisley, Scotland), and *denim,* a fabric that originally came from Nîmes, France, and was therefore characterized as being *de Nîmes.* Again, sometimes the process goes the other way around and places receive their names from those of foods. The linguistic results, as we'll see in a moment, include *Bethlehem, Marathon,* and possibly *Chicago.* But first, some of the stories behind the many foods named after people.

Military Leaders and Common Soldiers

Napoleons, those rich bars of flaky puff pastry and custard, call to mind "the little corporal," of course. And the savory *soubise* sauce honors another French officer,

Charles de Rohan, prince de Soubise, the general who is credited with creating this blend of strained onions in butter and creamy béchamel. (It's more likely that this sauce was invented by Soubise's chef, Marin, widely regarded as one of the greatest of the eighteenth century.) French military officers must have eaten very well indeed, judging by the other foods that bear their names: The creation of the *mirepoix,* a mixture of finely chopped and sautéed onions, carrots, celery, and other vegetables, is credited to the personal cook of a French field marshal, the duc de Lévis-Mirepoix. And seventeenth-century French army officer César de Choiseul, comte du Plessis-Praslin, gained culinary immortality for his association with the confection of almonds or pecans stirred into a boiling sugar syrup, the *praline.*

The urge to gloat over military victories appears to have inspired other food words as well. A possible case in point is *mayonnaise.* Many authorities believe the first batch of this mixture of egg yolks, oil, and seasonings was whipped up to celebrate the 1756 French capture of *Mahón,* a city on the Spanish isle of Minorca, by forces under Louis-François-Armand de Vignerot du Plessis, duc de Richelieu. Besides enjoying a reputation as a skillful military leader, the duke was also widely known as a bon vivant with the odd habit of inviting his guests to dine in the nude. The duke—or more likely, his personal chef—is credited with inventing this edible monument to that strategic success.

Chicken marengo salutes another French military victory. Napoleon is said to have dined on this dish flavored with tomatoes, mushrooms, onion, garlic, olives, and white wine while celebrating his victory over the Austrians at the northern Italian village of Marengo.[1]

Fifteen years later Napoleon was trounced at Waterloo by British forces under the command of Arthur Wellesley, first duke of Wellington. The jubilant English expressed their gratitude by naming several items of clothing after him, including waterproof Wellington boots. They also christened in his honor the hearty dish of beef, liver pâté, bacon, and brandy in a puff-pastry shell now known as *beef Wellington.* A respectful nod to the nineteenth-century Italian general Giuseppe Garibaldi, whose nationalist army of "Redshirts" helped unite Italy, is contained in the name of the British cookie called a *garibaldi.* Because they're currant-filled, these sweets also go by the descriptive but considerably less appetizing name of *squashed-fly biscuits.*

Echoes of ancient military leaders' names are occasionally audible in modern kitchens. *Pompey's head,* a roll of ground meat in a tomato-and-green-pepper sauce, today commemorates the Roman general Gnaeus Pompeius Magnus, also known as Pompey the Great, who was known for having an exceptionally broad head.

---

[1] A persistent folk etymology holds that even Napoleon's horse, Nichol, earned a place in gastronomic history, having bequeathed his name to the bread called *pumpernickel.* According to this fanciful story, this coarse, dark loaf served as *pain pour Nichol,* or "bread for Nichol," during the long march to Moscow. Actually, the etymology of *pumpernickel* is probably much naughtier. (See Chapter 2.)

Pompey's archrival, Julius Caesar, is indirectly commemorated in the name of the kitchen staple *sherry*. The name *sherry* is an alteration of the name of the Spanish town where this fortified wine was originally produced, *Jerez de la Frontera. Jerez*, in turn, derives from the town's ancient name, *urbs Caesaris*, Latin for "town of Caesar." Eventually *Jerez* found its way into English as *sherris*, but, being misunderstood as a plural, this word was eventually shortened to *sherry*.[2] (A *Caesar salad*, however, honors restaurateur Caesar Cardini, who invented it in Tijuana, Mexico, in 1924. Cardini's original recipe included romaine, garlic, croutons, Parmesan cheese, boiled eggs, olive oil, and Worcestershire sauce. He was said to be staunchly against the inclusion of anchovies in this mixture, contending that the Worcestershire sauce was what actually provided that faint fishy flavor.)

Common soldiers are commemorated in such names as *poor knights' pudding* or *poor knights of Windsor*, a British version of what Americans call French toast. An economical yet hearty meal for a poor soldier, this dish features a spread of jam or syrup sandwiched between slices of batter-soaked, skillet-browned bread. In Germany, a similar version goes by the name *arme Ritter*, or "poor knights."[3]

---

[2] For more about the many other food words formed by mistake, see Chapter 3.

[3] In France, French toast goes by the name *pain perdu*, or "lost bread." The *pain*, or "bread," in its name is related to *companion*, someone who

One more food has its origins in soldiers' fare: *Salisbury steaks*. These patties of finely chopped beef and seasonings are the namesake of Dr. James Henry Salisbury, who during the Civil War promoted a similar version as a "meat cure" for soldiers who were suffering from "camp diarrhea." A staunch advocate of shredding *all* food to make it more digestible, Dr. Salisbury prescribed a regimen of eating beef three times a day, chased with cup after cup of hot water. The doctor's own health apparently didn't suffer from this regimen—he died at the respectable old age of eighty-two.

Chefs and Restaurateurs

Several recipes bestow credit directly on the inventive chefs and restaurant owners who created them. *Fettuccine Alfredo* bears the name of Italian restaurateur Alfredo Di Lelio, who is said to have composed this dish of noodles, butter, cream, and Parmesan cheese in 1914 in the hope of perking up his wife's appetite while she was recuperating from childbirth. His creation enjoyed a publicity bonanza thirteen years later, after it became a favorite of actors Douglas Fairbanks and Mary Pickford. And in 1926, when a Los Angeles restaurant owner with the all-American name of Bob Cobb was

eats "bread with" someone else. *Perdu,* or "lost," is etymologically linked to the utter "loss" that is *perdition.* In any case, the name *pain perdu* apparently refers either to the fact that the bread is smothered or "lost" under other ingredients or that this recipe provides a handy way to use up French bread, which often goes stale before it's used up.

looking for a way to use up leftovers, he threw together some avocado, celery, tomato, chives, watercress, hard-boiled eggs, chicken, bacon, and Roquefort cheese and named it after himself: *Cobb salad*. Several chefs, meanwhile, have tried to claim credit for the most famous sweet in all literature, the *madeleine*. Culinary legend credits this elegant little cake's creation to a nineteenth-century French chef and pastry maker, Madeleine Palmier. (The name *Madeleine* itself derives from *Mary Magdalene*. Usually portrayed in art as a symbol of weepy penitence, her name also led to our modern term for "mawkish or weepy sentimentality," *maudlin*.)

Savvy chefs and restaurateurs sometimes name a creation after a favorite or particularly well-heeled customer. That seems to have happened several times, in fact, at the legendary New York restaurant Delmonico's. According to one story, a regular customer named Mrs. LeGrand Benedict complained to staffers that she was tired of the same old menu. The maître d' asked what she'd prefer, and their conversation led to the famous combination of English muffins, ham or Canadian bacon, a poached egg, and a dollop of hollandaise known as *eggs Benedict*.

Another time, a wealthy shipping magnate named Benjamin Wenburg brought the Delmonico's chef a recipe for an extraordinarily rich dish of lobster in a cream sauce with sherry, egg yolks, cayenne pepper, and other seasonings. The chef tried it out, the cholesterol-choked result became an instant hit, and the grateful chef returned the favor by dubbing the dish *lobster*

Wenburg. Things ended badly, however: Wenburg allegedly found himself involved in a drunken brawl in the restaurant's posh dining room, and the management retaliated by changing the entrée's name to *lobster Newburg.*

Many culinary historians credit the Delmonico's menu with yet another addition to the gastronomic lexicon: one story has it that when Foxhall P. Keene, the well-heeled son of Wall Street broker James R. Keene, dreamed aloud to the Delmonico's chef about a dish of chicken in a pimento-studded cream sauce, the chef obliged and shrewdly named the result *chicken à la Keene,* an appellation that eventually evolved into the more regal-sounding *chicken à la king.*

Earlier this century, the chef at the New Orleans restaurant Antoine's created an exceedingly rich dish of oysters baked with bread crumbs, herbs, butter, and white wine and named it *oysters Rockefeller.* (*Rockefeller,* by the way, is a food name of sorts, deriving as it does from the Dutch *roggenfelder,* or "rye field.") Another New Orleans dining establishment, Brennan's, is home to what may be the only food ever named after an awning salesman: In the early 1950s, Chef Paul Blange created a recipe for sliced bananas in a warm, sweetened sauce of butter, rum, and banana cordial poured over vanilla ice cream. He dubbed the dessert *bananas Foster* in honor of a regular customer, Richard Foster, owner of the nearby Foster Awning Company.

Sometimes culinary creations are lovingly dedicated to a relative. For some reason, this is particularly true in the case of candies. For example, contrary to what many people think, the candy bar called a *Baby Ruth* isn't an homage to the Sultan of Swat, George Herman "Babe" Ruth.[4] In his enlightening book *Devious Derivations*, for example, linguistic sleuth Hugh Rawson argues that the name *Baby Ruth* honors the granddaughter of the candy's original manufacturer, George Williamson, but apparently that's not the real story either. According to the manufacturer, this peanut-and-caramel-filled chocolate bar commemorates the young daughter of President Grover Cleveland, born during one of his terms in the White House. The daughter of another confectioner, Leo Hirschfield of New York, is commemorated in the name of the candy he invented: his daughter's real name was Clara, but she went by the nickname Tootsie, and in her honor her doting father named his chewy chocolate logs *Tootsie Rolls*. Yet another New York candy maker, Philip Silverstein, named his nut-and-raisin-filled chocolate squares after his daughter, who—for reasons that don't seem difficult to imagine—went by the nickname *Chunky*.

Other Occupations

Many foods commemorate working people of all kinds, reflecting in their names a host of various occupations and trades. Shepherds' humble fare inspired not only that staple of English pub grub, *shepherd's pie*, but also

---

[4] By the way, there once was a country called Swat, now part of east Pakistan, which indeed had a sultan—hence the ballplayer's nickname.

Hungarian *goulash*. This paprika-seasoned mixture of meat and vegetables takes its name from the Hungarian word *gulyás*, or "herdsman's" stew. Food prepared "hunter style" makes plentiful use of mushrooms, easily available to hunters trekking through forests. In Italy, such *cacciatore* dishes feature mushrooms, onions, tomatoes, and herbs, while in France, they go by the name *chasseur* and include a brown sauce of mushrooms, white wine, and shallots. (Both *cacciatore* and *chasseur* literally mean "hunter" and are linguistic cousins of the English *catch* and *chase*.)

A dish described as *meunière*, such as the lightly flour-dusted and sautéed *trout meunière* (or, in Italian, *trota alla mugnaia*), is prepared the way a "miller's wife" would. A descendant of the Latin *molīnārius*, or "miller," *meunière* is a relative of such "whirling," "grinding," and "milling" words as *maelstrom* (literally a "whirl stream" in Dutch), *miller, molar,* and *meal* (the powdery kind). These words are also the etymological kin of the trademark name for one of the handiest kitchen gadgets ever invented, that handheld, rotating grater called a *Mouli.*

Farming is celebrated in the Dutch name for raisins in brandy, *boerenjongens*—literally, "farmer boys"—and their apricots-in-brandy equivalent *boerenmeisje,* "farmer girls." (The *boer,* or "farmer," in these names, incidentally, is a relative of the English *boor*—just one of several pejorative words that originally specified country folk, such as *villain,* which comes from the Latin *villa,* or "country house." The word *boer,* or "farmer," also applied specifically to the Dutch settlers in South Africa and appears in the *Boer War* between those colonists and the British in 1899. It's also a relative of the German name *Bauer*, which means "farmer" and is part of a German idiom meaning "to burp": literally, *Bäuerchen machen* means "to make a little farmer."

Other food names come from those whose jobs take them to sea. *Marinara* describes something cooked "sailor" style and belongs to a whole fleet of seagoing words that include *marine, mermaid,* and the briny solution used for pickling, a *marinade*. Similarly, the fish stew cooked in wine sauce called *matelote* comes from the French for "sailor," *matelot*, a derivative of either the Old French for "bunkmate" or the Old Norse *mötunautr*, "messmate." *Navy beans*, the white legumes also known as *Yankee beans*, are so called because they've been a significant part of the U.S. Navy's bean cuisine ever since the mid–nineteenth century. And the *shaddock*, a variety of citrus similar to a grapefruit, is named after an English sea captain. According to a 1707 history of Jamaica, "The seed of this was first brought to Barbados by one Captain Shaddock, Commander of an East-India Ship, who touch'd at that Island in his Passage to England, and left the Seed there."

Then there's the Italian *pollo alla scarpariello*, or "chicken shoemaker's style," little bits of tender chicken meat on the bone that are traditionally picked off and eaten with the fingers. As Jay Jacobs explains in his fascinating book *The Eaten Word*, this name apparently stems from the way enthusiastic diners' fingers keep flying to their mouths while eating this dish—much like those of a shoemaker as he toils away with a mouthful of tacks, continually reaching to his lips for another.

Finally, a few foods are named for those who make their living outside the law. *Arni kleftico,* a Greek dish of lamb cooked in a foil packet with celery, onions, and potatoes, is a name that recalls how roaming Greek bandits would steal townspeople's food, then cook it in paper packets to avoid being detected by its aroma. Literally, *arni kleftico* means "stolen lamb," *kleftico* being a linguistic relative of the English *kleptomaniac.* Then there's *pasta putanesca,* or "whore's pasta," with its hearty sauce of tomatoes, garlic, capers, anchovies, and olives. Supposedly originating in the slums of Naples, its name alludes to the fact that this dish can be thrown together so quickly that even a busy prostitute can whip up a batch of it between clients.

Artists and Their Art

Culinary artists sometimes pay tribute to artists in other fields by naming a special recipe in their honor. Many such foods commemorate opera singers, traditionally known for their robust appetites and lusty appreciation for sumptuous meals. Several foods have a *Melba* in their name, an affectionate reference to the world-famous soprano Dame Nellie Melba. Born Helen Porter Mitchell, she adopted the stage name Nellie Melba in honor of her hometown of Melbourne, Australia. Legendary French chef Auguste Escoffier is traditionally credited with inventing the luscious dessert of poached peaches, raspberry sauce, and ice cream known as *peach Melba,* which the smitten chef named in her honor. Years later, when the singer was suffering from ill health, Escoffier created for her the crisp, easily digestible dry bread now familiar to millions of dieters as *Melba toast.* The beloved diva also inspired the name of *strawberries Melba*—vanilla ice cream smothered in strawberry puree—and *Melba garniture*—small tomatoes stuffed with chicken, truffles, and mushrooms, smothered in a velouté, then sprinkled with bread crumbs and browned in Madeira or port wine sauce.

Gioacchino Antonio Rossini, the nineteenth-century Italian composer of the operas *The Barber of Seville* and *William Tell,* also lives on in the name of one of the richest and most expensive entrées on any menu, *tournedos à la Rossini.* Created at the composer's request at a popular Parisian restaurant, these thick, fat-wrapped rounds of tenderloin are served on fried bread and topped with liver pâté and a brown sauce of wine and truffles. (Technically, *tournedos* is both the singular and plural form, so there's no such thing as one *tournedo.* That's because the word *tournedos* is a compound of French *tourner,* "to turn," and *dos,* or "back."[5])

But why a name that means "turn the back"? Experts are divided on the answer. Some say the name de-

---

[5] *Tourner* is also related to several "turning" words that include the English *turn, contour, detour,* and *tour de force. Dos* is a linguistic cousin of the

rives from the fact that the beef filets cook quickly and are "done on one side before the cook has time to turn back around." A more colorful explanation, however, appears in the story of Rossini's original request for this unusual dish. When the great composer first suggested this odd combination of ingredients, the horrified maître d'hôtel replied that it sounded completely unpresentable. "Very well, then," the composer replied, "don't let us see you do it. I'll *turn my back*"—or, in French, *tourne le dos*.

According to another culinary tradition, Italian opera tenor Enrico Caruso hit a gastronomic high note one evening when he tossed together some spaghetti with chicken livers and tomatoes, and dubbed this combination *spaghetti Caruso*. Another chicken-and-pasta dish, with mushrooms and almonds in a cheese-topped cream sauce, *chicken Tetrazzini*, commemorates Luisa Tetrazzini, a well-fed Italian coloratura who enjoyed enormous popularity in this country at the turn of the century.

Some dishes serve as edible applause for stars of the theater and stage. The flaming, thin dessert pancakes called *crêpes suzettes* are said to honor the French actress Suzanne Reichenberg. When ballerina Anna Pavlova paid a visit to Australia in the 1920s, a star-

---

dorsal fin on a fish's "back" and *dossier*, originally a large bundle of papers supposedly so named either because it was so thick it bulged like a "back," or because it bore a distinctive label on the back of it. These words are also kin to that perennial square-dance favorite, *do-si-do*, from French *dos-à-dos*, or "back to back."

struck (or perhaps just savvy) chef whipped up a fluffy dessert featuring a meringue in the shape of a dancer's tutu, topped with luscious fruits. The *pavlova,* also affectionately known as a *pav,* remains enormously popular Down Under. A flamboyant American singer and actress of the end of the nineteenth century, Lillian Russell, bequeathed her name to the dessert now called a *Lillian Russell*—half a cantaloupe filled with ice cream.

The palette of one visual artist meets the palate of discerning diners in the form of *veal* or *tuna carpaccio.* This dish of thinly sliced raw beef or tuna is a kind of homage to Venetian Renaissance artist Vittore Carpaccio, whose work is often distinguished by a splash of bright red.

Literary artists occasionally appear on menus as well. The German fish dish known as *Schillerlocken* is named for the late-eighteenth-century German romanticist Johann Christoph Friedrich von Schiller. These filets curl up tightly when smoked, which apparently reminded Schiller's fans of the writer's famous flowing locks.

Likewise, an order of *Châteaubriand* honors the French novelist and politician Vicomte François René de Châteaubriand, whose moody, egotistical works published in the early nineteenth century are considered forerunners of the Romantic literary movement. In 1802, the author supposedly dined at a Parisian restaurant to celebrate the publication of his widely acclaimed *Le Génie du christianisme,* or *The Genius of Christianity.* The admiring proprietor served him an entrée created especially for the occasion—a slice of tenderloin cooked between two flank steaks that were seared and then discarded, leaving the tenderloin rare and juicy inside. According to culinary tradition, this symbolized the crucifixion of Jesus between two thieves. Many experts believe, however, that this whole story is fanciful and that the entrée bears Châteaubriand's name because it was invented by the writer's personal chef.

Writers' literary creations likewise live on in the names of various dishes. For example, *apple Charlotte* is an adaptation of an earlier version called *fruit Charlotte*, a dessert that may honor a character from a wildly popular novel by Johann Wolfgang von Goethe. Many historians believe this dessert was inspired by Charlotte Buff, the "Lotte" in Goethe's epistolary novel *Die Leiden des jungen Werthers*, or *The Sorrows of Young Werther*. Published in 1774, this partly autobiographical book is the story of Lotte's would-be suitor, a sensitive, artistic young man whom Goethe describes as "gifted with deep, pure sentiment and penetrating intelligence, who loses himself in fantastic dreams and undermines himself with speculative thought until finally, torn by hopeless passions, especially by infinite love, he shoots himself in the head." The heroine of this cheery tale, at any rate, is memorialized in a heavenly dessert of sautéed, spiced apples in a shell of buttered bread.[6]

---

[6] The great French chef Marie-Antoine Carême is credited with inventing a different dessert called a *charlotte*, a ladyfinger shell filled with

The strapping hero Stromboli in Carlo Collodi's *Pinocchio* apparently inspired the name of a sandwich of pizza dough folded over pepperoni and mozzarella, the stromboli. (The name, in turn, may be a nod to the island of Stromboli, off the southern Italian coast, which is famous for its active volcano.) Likewise, *Harlequin,* a stock character of classic Italian comedy, inspired a French word for "a mishmash of leftovers," *arlequin* — a reference to the similarity to the food's jumbled appearance and the character's patchwork or diamond-patterned tights. The liquor-soaked cake called a *baba* may also have a literary source. The story goes that Poland's King Stanisław Leszczyński invented the dessert in the early eighteenth century by dipping a stale cake into rum. Enchanted with the recent appearance of the first European translation of *A Thousand and One Nights,* the king named his treat after the character of Ali Baba. That's the story, anyway. However, other evidence suggests that this cake's name comes from the Polish *baba,* or "old woman," which would make it a linguistic relative of the Russian *babushka,* which means "grandmother" or, literally, "little old woman," and now also designates the triangular scarf worn by a *babushka.*

Bavarian cream and topped with whipped-cream rosettes. At the time, he was in Moscow, cooking for Russia's Tsar Alexander. Perhaps homesick, he dubbed his creation *charlotte parisienne.* Later, however, he did the politically astute thing and changed the name to *charlotte russe* in honor of his employer.

(Occasionally this process works in reverse, and a fictitious character winds up being named for a food. That's what happened with *Tartuffe*, the title character in the comedy about a religious hypocrite by Jean-Baptiste Poquelin, otherwise known as Molière. The word *tartuffe* in English now denotes any hypocrite, especially a religious one, and the useful but underused word *tartuffery* denotes vain and empty self-righteousness. The name *Tartuffe* itself derives from the Italian word for "truffle," *tartufo*, a descendant of the Latin *terrae tuber*—literally, "truffle of the earth.")

Royalty, Government Officials, and Nations

Many food names offer a culinary curtsy to various unnamed members of royalty and their taste for the sweet and sumptuous. There's the decadent *fruit salad tsarina*, with its mixed fruit soaked in sugar and the cumin-flavored liqueur kümmel, then topped with pineapple ice cream; *duchess potatoes*, pureed with yolks and butter, then shaped and browned; and *riz à l'impératrice*, a rich rice pudding that also includes vanilla custard, whipped cream, and kirsch-soaked crystallized fruit, which, as its French name indicates, is "rice as the empress likes it." Then there are the lemon and almond tarts called *mademoiselles d'honneur*, or "maids of honor." Tradition holds that these treats were invented by a young lady-in-waiting named Anne Boleyn in the hope of impressing King Henry VIII.

Royals from the East also inhabit a few food names. The name for dried white grapes, *sultanas*, means "sultan's wives" in Italian, a nod to the fact these fruits came originally from Turkey. Likewise, recipes *à la sultane* allude to the eastern origins of their key ingredient, pistachios. (*Pistachio*, incidentally, comes from a Middle Persian word for this nut.)

Still other food names refer to specific members of royalty or nobility. In fact, many a marquis has left his mark on our gastronomic vocabulary. The Italian marquis Muzio Frangipani supposedly invented an almond-scented perfume that was all the rage in sixteenth-century Paris. Parisian pastry cooks tried to cash in on the perfume's popularity (and the marquis's reputation) with a new custard made with crushed almonds, which they christened with this lilting name.

The beloved French cream sauce *béchamel* is named for the high-rolling financier and passionate gourmet who became the royal superintendent of the kitchen of Louis XIV, the Marquis Louis de Béchameil. And the purée of shallots, mushrooms, and herbs called a *duxelles* honors yet another marquis, the Marquis d'Uxelles, who had the great good fortune to employ its inventor, one of history's greatest chefs, François Pierre de La Varenne. (The modern version of this sauce, however, bears only a passing resemblance to the original, which included egg yolks, cream, butter, and a complex boullion of vegetables, wines, and, according to one source, "old hens, and old partridges."[7])

An English noble bequeathed his name to one of the most popular repasts in the world. In 1762, so the story goes, John Montagu, fourth earl of Sandwich, was so engrossed in one of his many all-night gambling sessions that he refused to break for a meal. Instead, he ordered an underling to bring him slices of cold roast and cheeses between two pieces of bread so he could keep one hand free for gambling. The incident became such a notorious example of the earl's excesses that soon people were referring to such handy snacks as *sandwiches*.

Another English earl, Charles Grey, served as prime minister under William IV and left a political legacy that included helping abolish slavery throughout the British Empire. However, he's probably better known today for lending his name to *Earl Grey tea*. According to tradition, the earl received the recipe for this exotically flavored brew sometime in the 1830s, a gift from a Chinese government official whose life had been saved by a British diplomat.

A few other foods boast a royal pedigree, but their noble lineage is tucked deep inside their names. Legend has it that it was once forbidden for anyone except a king to snip off a sprig of *basil*. The aromatic herb's

---

[7] Hens and partridges are also key ingredients in another fit-for-royalty food, the German sausage called a *Königswurst,* or "king's sausage," also known as a *saucisse royale* in French.

name supposedly reflects this prohibition, for *basil* comes from the Greek *basilikon,* or "royal." Thus the name of this spice is a linguistic relative of *basilica* (originally, a "royal palace"), as well as the masculine names *Basil* and *Vasily,* both of which mean "king." These words are also kin to *basiliskos,* or "little king," the ancient Greeks' name for a legendary serpent that had a cock's head, a dragon's tail, the wings of a bird, and deadly breath. Its name alludes to its crownlike crest, as does the name of the real-life lizard called a *basilisk.*

Germans, meanwhile, nibble a pear they call an "emperor's pear," or *Kaiserbirne,* a name which, like *Czar,* is a descendant of the ancient emperor name *Caesar.* Another imperial appellation for a fruit: *king-apple,* an early English name for the pineapple. The name for this then-unfamiliar import from the tropics is said to have been inspired by its stiff crest of leaves, which resemble a crown—though its large size was probably also a factor.

Another royal food is the soft, juicy pear called a *bergamot,* which gets its name from the Turkish for "prince's pear," *beg-armudu.* It's worth noting, by the way, that the Turkish *beg,* or "prince," in *beg-armudu* also led to the English word *bey,* an honorific variously applied to any provincial governor of the Ottoman Empire, and also a title designating various Middle Eastern dignitaries.

Speaking of government officials, some food names allude to politicians or political jobs. Despite his years of government service, nineteenth-century Russian diplomat Count Paul Stroganoff is now best remembered for the dish of beef sautéed with onions, mushrooms, and sour cream that bears his name, *beef Stroganoff*. Stroganoff's compatriot, Russian statesman Count Karl Nesselrode, likewise may be less renowned for his political achievements than for the *Nesselrode*, a cold pudding of custard with chestnut purée, candied fruit, and rum, the invention of which is credited to the politician's personal chef, Monsieur Mouy. Other governmental food names include *diplomat pudding, chancellor's pudding,* and *cabinet pudding*, names applied to several recipes of liqueur-soaked ladyfingers, custard, whipped cream, and dried or candied fruit. The name *mandarin orange*, a citrus fruit originally found in the Far East, was inspired by the brilliant robes of the same color worn by Chinese government officials. Then there's *hunkyar begendi*, a Turkish dish of puréed eggplant mixed with white sauce and grated cheese. Its name refers to a type of Turkish government official called a *hunkyar*—literally, the name translates as "the hunkyar was pleased."

Sometimes food names commemorate not just governments but entire nations. In Britain, for example, the firm-fleshed rutabaga is called a *swede*, this vegetable having been introduced to Scotland from Scandinavia in the late eighteenth century. (The name *rutabaga* itself comes from a Swedish dialectical term, *rotabagge*, or "baggy root.") Similarly, the medley of fruits or vegetables called a *macédoine* takes its name from the French word for "Macedonia" because of the diverse ethnic makeup of Alexander the Great's Macedonian empire in the Balkans.

Other foods named for nations include *steak tartare,* which commemorates the fierce *Tatars* and their practice of shredding meat with a knife and eating it raw. The pungent combination of mayonnaise, capers, pickles, and onions known as *tartar sauce* is also said to be named after these hot-tempered, savage people. Similiarly, *Shawnee cakes* (also called *johnnycakes*) recall these corn pancakes' American Indian origins.

Finally, there's *walnut.* This food name is connected to the fact that the Saxons who invaded England referred to any native Celt there as a "foreigner" or, in their language, a *wealh.* Over time, *wealh* became the Old English *wælisc,* which eventually evolved into the modern English *Welsh.* Likewise, noting the difference between walnuts and the more familiar hazelnuts that grew plentifully on the continent, the invaders considered these larger specimens "foreign nuts" or "Celtic nuts." Their name for this nut evolved into the Old English *wealhhnutu,* meaning "foreign [or Celtic] nut," which eventually became the modern English *walnut.* Incidentally, the Romans referred to the foreign-looking walnut as the "French nut," or *nux gallica,* and a linguistic shell of that name remains visible in the French dialect terms for "walnut," *gaog* and *gok.*

The Other Way Around: People Named After Foods

Occasionally people are named after foods. From the Latin word *cicer,* or "chickpea," for example, comes the

name of the greatest orator of ancient Rome, *Cicero,*
whose name supposedly was inspired because of a
similar-looking wart at the end of his nose. (Prominent
physical characteristics inspired many other Roman
names: The greatest poet of his generation, Ovid, was
called Publius Ovidius *Naso.* The last of these names, a
relative of the English *nasal,* comes from the Latin for
"nose.")[8] At any rate, the Latin word *cicer,* or "chickpea," found its way into Old French as *chiche.* Speakers
of Middle English adopted this name for the legume
and tacked on a redundant *pease,* or "pea" at the end of
it. It wasn't long before the resulting compound transformed into a more familiar-sounding name *chickpea.*

Speaking of chickpeas, another of the Latin *cicer's*
descendants played a pivotal role in the bloody Sicilian
uprising against French rule in 1282. Sicilian rebels,
who had orders to kill every French person on sight,
faced the problem of determining who was and wasn't
French. So they commanded every stranger they met
to say *"cecceri,"* an Italian dialect expression for "chickpeas." Strangers who failed to pronounce it correctly
were killed.[9]

---

[8] Similarly, the *Crassus* in Marcus Licinius Crassus, who was once
Rome's principal landowner, literally means "fat." The Latin *crassus* in
the sense of "dense" also led to our own word for someone who is
"crude" or "lacking in refinement." Another famous name that means
"fat," incidentally, is *Tolstoy.*

[9] Such telltale linguistic giveaways, called *shibboleths,* are first described
in the biblical account of how the Gileadites identified their enemies,

In addition to individuals named after foods, some groups have foods in their names as well. In the 1760s, *macaroni* became another word for "a fashionable English dandy." The reference is to the Macaroni Club, whose members affected Continental manners, style, and taste, wore their hair in long curls, and dined on foreign cuisine, including macaroni, which was still an exotic Italian import. "There is indeed a kind of animal," sniffed *Oxford Magazine* in 1770, "neither male nor female, a thing of the neuter gender, lately started up amongst us. It is called a Macaroni. It talks without meaning, it smiles without pleasantry, it eats without appetite, it rides without exercise, it wenches without passion." (Shortly thereafter, the British introduced the tune "Yankee Doodle" to America to mock the colonists; the part about Mr. Doodle sticking a feather in his cap and calling it macaroni was actually a stinging reference to the ragged, poorly clad local troops.)

Similarly, the Yeomen of the Guard, the protectors of the British monarch, got their nickname, *Beefeaters,*

the Ephraimites, by demanding that they pronounce the Hebrew word *shibboleth,* which could mean either "rushing water" or "an ear of corn": "Then Gilead cut Ephraim off from the fords of the Jordan, and whenever an Ephraimite fugitive said, 'Let me cross,' the men of Gilead asked him, 'Are you an Ephraimite?' If he answered 'No,' they said, 'Then say "Shibboleth." ' He would say 'Sibboleth,' since he could not pronounce the word correctly. Thereupon they seized and slaughtered him by the fords of the Jordan." In English, *shibboleth* has come to mean any custom, practice, or pronunciation that identifies someone as an outsider.

from a rather derisive seventeenth-century term for servants who are especially well fed, as compared to the *hlāfǣtan,* or "bread eaters," commonly applied to more hardworking, ordinary underlings. (For more about *hlāfǣtan* and their relationship to such words as *lord, lady,* and *loaf,* see Chapter 6.) Incidentally, the French sometimes mockingly apply the term *rosbif,* or "roast beef," to an Englishman—although this appellation could just as well be a dig at the notoriously uninspired nature of British cooking.

Less obvious examples of people named for what they eat—or allegedly eat—occur in the cases of several American Indian nations. The name *Mohawk* comes from an Algonquian term meaning "they eat animate things." The Dakota tribe called the *Winnebago* by a name thought to mean "fish eaters," and the *Natchitoches* have a name that in Caddo means either "chestnut eaters" or "pawpaw eaters." And the tribe known as the *Adirondack* has a name that derives from the Mohawks' sneering epithet for them, *Hatiróntaks*—literally, "they eat trees."

Tasty Toponyms

Many food names are toponyms, deriving from the names of places. There are the obvious examples, of course, such as the many cheeses named for the towns or regions where they're produced: *Colby,* from Colby, Wisconsin; *Monterey jack,* from the California coastal town of Monterey; *Cheddar,* which originated in a village of the same name in southwest England; and the cheese first

116

produced in the Dutch town of *Edam,* a name that has prompted many a wag to joke that Edam cheese is "made" backwards. (The English cheese known as *yarg,* on the other hand, really is spelled backwards. The name of this mild white cheese pays a sort of backhanded compliment to its inventors, Jennifer and Allan Gray.)

The physical appearances of other edibles suggest an association with various places. *Baked Alaska* is a dessert of sponge cake and ice cream covered with a meringue that's browned so briefly the ice cream stays cold. This dish supposedly was invented by Delmonico's chef Charles Ranhofer in 1869, to commemorate the purchase of the Alaska territory two years earlier. (In Ranhofer's own cookbook, he calls this dessert *Alaska, Florida.* The French had already perfected a version of this dish they called an *omelette norvégienne,* or "Norwegian omelette"; they, in turn, are said to have adopted the idea for a hot-meringue-and-frozen-ice-cream treat from one traditionally prepared in China.)

A salad dressing perhaps named for its resemblance to a place is *Thousand Island,* which is filled with bits of green olives, peppers, pickles, onions, hard-cooked eggs, and other finely chopped ingredients. Culinary lore has it that this chunky dressing commemorates the Thousand Islands in the Saint Lawrence River.

A little more etymological detective work reveals other tasty toponyms. The chewy yeast roll called a *bialy* is named for the Polish city where it was invented, *Białystok.* And the creamy seafood soup called a *bisque* is said to have originated near the Bay of Biscay, which extends along the coasts of northern Spain and western France.

Fig Newtons might just as easily have been named *Fig Marbleheads, Fig Swampscotts, Fig Shirleys,* or *Fig Shrewsburys.* When the Kennedy Biscuit Works of Cambridgeport, Massachusetts, needed a name for this chewy cookie, company officials decided to combine the word *fig* plus the name of some nearby town in the hope of drumming up local business. The town of *Newton* won out over the other possibilities.

(Another Massachusetts landmark appears in the name of America's favorite cookie: Around 1930, a baker at an inn on the outskirts of Whitman, Massachusetts, began adding bits of chocolate to her basic butter cookie. As the reputation of these delectable treats grew, so did the name of the place where she worked, the *Toll House* Inn.)

By some accounts, the German city of *Hamburg* (a name that comes from the Old German *Hammaburg,* or "forest city") is the original home of the ever-popular *hamburger.* Supposedly this recipe traveled to the United States along with a wave of German immigrants in the 1880s. Here it became known as a *hamburger steak,* a name sometimes shortened to plain old *hamburg.* Other cities, however, also lay claim to the invention of this round of pounded beefsteak. Among the contenders: the city of Hamburg, New York, where two refreshment vendors at the 1885 Erie County Fair supposedly ran out of pork for making sandwiches and came up with this now ubiquitous beef sandwich.

Similarly, many sausages are named for their cities of origin. *Wienerwurst,* literally, "Vienna sausage," wound up in English as *wiener.* The *frankfurter* originally was a specialty of Frankfurt, Germany. Two German Americans usually get the credit (or the blame) for popularizing this cylinder stuffed with ground animal parts: Antoine Feuchtwanger, who settled in Saint Louis, and Charles Feltman, an entrepreneur who introduced them to Coney Island, where they were also called *red hots.* As for *hot dog,* one persistent legend holds that this name had its origins in a turn-of-the-century cartoon by a popular cartoonist named Tad Dorgan. The story goes that Dorgan drew a frankfurter so as to resemble a dachshund on a long bun. Supposedly it was a visual pun playing upon both the idea that this particular breed was a symbol for things German, and the public's suspicion that this food contained meat from other than barnyard animals. Only thing is, no such cartoon has ever been found.

However, there was some truth to the dog-meat rumor, according to David K. Barnhart and Allan A. Metcalf, authors of *America in So Many Words.* They point out that an 1836 newspaper article noted that "Sausages have fallen in price one half, in New York, since the dog killers have commenced operations." A few years later, Yale University students jokingly called those sausages *dogs* and dubbed their favorite local lunch wagon "The Kennel Club." Soon they added the adjective *hot,* and eventually this more American-sounding name won out over *frankfurter.* (In any case, suspicions about ingredients were so widespread that in 1913 the Coney Island Chamber of Commerce banned the term *hot dog* from signs. When it was clear that *hot dog* had caught on anyway and no amount of linguistic legislating could prohibit its usage, the chamber rescinded the rule.)

Sometimes when people encounter strange foods, they name them for the faraway places that export them. *Laitue romaine,* or "Roman lettuce," was applied to an exotic leafy vegetable that first arrived in France having been shipped through Rome from the eastern Mediterranean. In English it became simply *romaine.* (Romaine also goes by the name *cos lettuce* because it originated on Cos, an Aegean island famous in antiquity as the home of the Greek physician Hippocrates.)

Similarly, the Germans dubbed the orange an *Apfelsine,* or "Chinese apple," because it came from the Far East. In Turkish, meanwhile, an orange is a *portukal,* named for the Portuguese traders who carried them. When a new, deep-orange-colored citrus fruit first found its way to Europe in the 1840s, the fact that it had come from the Moroccan city of Tangier prompted the British to call it a *tangerine. Mocha,* originally a bitter coffee and now a coffee-and-chocolate flavoring, is so named because for a long time it was exported only from the Southern Yemen city of the same name.

The herb the Romans called *ligusticum* (literally "herb from Liguria," a coastal region of northeast Italy), underwent a complex etymological evolution, appearing in Medieval Latin as *levistica* and in Old French as *levesche,* which eventually became the English *lovage*. The ancient Romans, meanwhile, seasoned their salads with a type of onion they called *caepa Ascalōnia*, or "onion of Ashkelon," a reference to the Mediterranean port city from which it came. This Latin name was the forerunner of the English *scallion*. The Old French version of this word is *eschaloigne*, and its diminutive, *eschalotte*, led to the English *shallot*.[10]

Similarly, the *currant* contains the image of a famous Greek seaport in its name: in Middle English, these small, seedless fruits were known as *raysons of coraunte*, or "raisins of Corinth," because that city once served as their major exporter. Incidentally, *currant*'s German cognate *Korinthe*, is part of an exquisitely evocative German term for "an exacting petty bureaucrat"—a *Korinthenkacker*, literally, is a "currant crapper." (Somewhat along the same lines is the picturesque English term for a "tightwad": *cumin splitter*, a direct translation of the Latin and Greek words for the same thing, *cuminisector* and *kuminopristes*.)

The geographical origins of the *peach* are also subtly betrayed in its name. Borrowed from the Old French *peche*, *peach* derives ultimately from the Latin for "peach tree," *persica*, an allusion to the fact that this fruit was thought to have originated in Persia. The name of the *rhubarb* plant is another case in point. It's thought to

---

[10] The *caepa*, or "onion," in *caepa Ascalōnia*, on the other hand, blossomed into the French word *ciboule*, or "scallion," as well as the Spanish for "onion," *cebolla*. In English, the Latin *caepa* evolved into the word for a smaller type of onion, *chive*.

come from a combination of the Greeks' word for the Volga River, *Rha,* with the Latin word *barbarum,* meaning "foreign" or "barbarous," rhubarb being native to the banks of the Volga, which lies in territory that both the Greeks and Romans considered "foreign."

The Volga isn't the only river embedded in our culinary vocabulary. When Spanish conquistadors chanced upon a Peruvian place named for the nearby *Rimac* river, they marveled at a new kind of fat, nutritious legume. The Europeans mangled that city's name, pronouncing it *Lima,* and applied that name to the beans that originated there. Another "river" flows through the word *tabasco.* Shortly after the Civil War, New Orleans banker Edmund McIhenny sought to rebuild his fortune by creating a piquant sauce made from chilies picked in an area near the *Tabasco* river in southern Mexico. This river's name, which in a native language means "damp earth," is now synonymous with the spicy condiment of salt, vinegar, and hot peppers.

In fact, several other spicy foods are namesakes of various places. *Jalapeños* are named for the old city of Jalapa, in east-central Mexico. *Cayenne* pepper, on the other hand, is so named because of a mistaken association with the capital of French Guiana, *Cayenne.* It was originally called a *quiínia,* or simply "hot pepper," in the native Tupi language of Brazil, but Europeans later mistakenly associated this word with the city. *Chili* peppers, however, aren't named for the South American country; the Aztecs called this pungent fruit a *chilli.* (The name apparently led to linguistic confusion of a different sort when such peppers were still considered a novelty in England, as noted in this exchange in William Thackeray's *Vanity Fair:* "'Try a chili with it, Miss Sharp,' said Joseph, really interested. 'A chili,' said Rebecca, gasping; 'oh yes!' She thought a chili was something cool, as its name imported.")

The Other Way Around: Places Named for Foods

Just as some people's names derive from the names of various foods, foods show up in place names as well. The city of *Saskatoon,* Saskatchewan, takes its name from a Cree term for a berry which, as a writer noted in 1894, is "very luscious fruit like a black currant and bilberry combined," the *saskatoon.* Similarly, the capital of Kazakhstan, *Alma-Ata,* has a name that literally means "father of apples," because of the abundance of apples growing there. And *Topeka,* Kansas, takes its name from the Dakota for "good place to dig potatoes."

From the Hebrew words *beth,* "house," and *lechem,* "bread," comes the name of the little town of *Bethlehem,* or "house of bread," which, in turn, eventually gave rise to an English word for "crazed confusion and uproar." In medieval London, the Hospital of Saint Mary of Bethlehem was converted into an asylum for the insane. Over time this grim institution came to be known simply as *Bethlehem,* then *Bethlem* and *Bedlem,* and eventually *Bedlam,* which in turn led to today's term for crazed noisiness and clamor.

Many people know that the 26-mile, 385-yard footrace called a *marathon* commemorates the heroic run of the ancient Greek messenger Pheidippides, who in 490 B.C. raced from Marathon to Athens to announce the Greeks' victory over the Persians. What most don't realize, though, is that *marathon* is the ancient Greek word for "fennel," and the city of *Marathon* was so named because this anise-flavored plant grew there in abundance.

America's third largest city smells faintly of onions, at least etymologically. Many authorities believe the name *Chicago* derives from an American Indian term meaning "place that stinks of wild onions." In *Made in America: An Informal History of the English Language in the United States*, Bill Bryson points out that American settlers did considerable casting about before settling on a proper spelling for the city's name. Over the years, it was variously rendered as "*Schuerkaigo, Psceschaggo, Shikkago, Tsckakko, Ztschaggo, Schecago, Shakakko, Stkanchango,* and almost any other remotely similar combination . . ."

Chicago in turn lent its redolent name to different types of food. Today *Chicago* is a slang term for "pineapple," as in *Chicago sundae*, a dessert featuring this fruit. And midwesterners sometimes refer to a jelly doughnut as a *Chicago*. In parts of Germany, by the way, *Berliner* can apply to a similar deep-fried, jelly-filled pastry as well as to an inhabitant of the city of Berlin. This double meaning led to no end of jokes after John F. Kennedy declared his solidarity with West Germans in June 1963 by proclaiming, "Ich bin ein Berliner."

5

BROKEN SUGAR
AND
FLYING PASTRIES

*Foods Named for What's Done to Them or
What They Do to Us*

A lot happens to food before it is eaten, and the names of many edibles reflect that fact. Some, such as *parsnips* and *grapes*, are named for how they're gathered. Others, such as *feta cheese, schnitzel, mozzarella,* and *pesto*, get their names from the ways in which they're sliced, cut, pounded, mashed, minced, or marinated. Still others come equipped with cooking instructions tucked right into their names, including *bouillabaisse, biscuit, ricotta, fritter,* and *chow mein.* Some food names, such as the British specialty *bubble and squeak,* offer a preview of what the food will do while it's being cooked, while the name *banger* warns of the consequences if these sausages are cooked improperly. The names *casserole, lasagna, paella,* and *chowder* indicate where to put these foods, while the names of the *endive* and *lobster thermidor* tell when to eat them, at least according to tradition. Many other food names reflect fanciful expectations about what that food will "do" after it's cooked, including *saltimbocca, vol-au-vent,* and the elegant-sounding term for one common vegetable that contains a hidden promise to prevent flatulence.

Foods That Are Gathered

Some foods' names refer to the instruments used to gather them. Because the ancient Romans used a two-pronged digging instrument called a *pastinum* to pry parsnips and carrots from the ground, they applied the name *pastinaca* to both these vegetables. This name moved into Old French as *pasnaie,* where it specified the parsnip, and eventually it found its way into English as *parsnip.* (In Russian, a parsnip is a *pasternak,* as in the name of Nobel Prize–winning poet and novelist Boris *Pasternak.*) Similarly, the word *spud,* a colloquial term for "potato," comes from the Middle English *spudde,* the short knife once used to dig them out.

Another food with a name inspired by the device used to gather it is the *grape*. In Old French, the word *grape* specified "a vine hook used to gather grapes"—a relative of the English *grapple*, originally a type of hook used in warfare to pull enemy ships close or tear away at the walls of a town under siege. Over time, the Old French *grape* came to mean "bunch of grapes," and only later did the word *grape* find its way into English as the name of a single one of these fruits, replacing the Old English name *winberige*, or "wine berry."

In the same way, several other languages' words for "grape" derive from earlier collective terms. From the Latin word for a "bunch of grapes," *racemus*, came the French word *raisin*, which likewise originally meant "bunch of grapes." Nowadays, however, the French use the term *grain de raisin* for "grape" and refer to a "bunch of grapes" as *une grappe de raisin*. Meanwhile, what we think of in English as "raisins" are known as *raisins secs* in France—in other words, "dry grapes." The *grapefruit*, meanwhile, is so named because, like grapes, it grows in clusters, albeit very large ones.

At least one type of food may be named for the fact that it is collected at all. Some etymologists suspect that because *legumes* must be collected by hand, this term for "peas" or "beans" may come from the Latin word *legere*, meaning "to gather." If that's the case, this would make *legume* an etymological relative of *collect*—literally, "gather together"—and possibly also several other languages' words for "vegetable," including the French *légume,* Italian *legume,* and Spanish *legumbre.*

Foods That Are Cut, Broken, Pierced, or Pounded

Many foods get their names from the ways in which they're cut, broken, stripped, shredded, or pierced during preparation. *Mozzarella* has a name that in Italian literally means "little cut," having descended from the Latin *mutilis,* meaning "mutilated." *Feta cheese,* on the other hand, derives from the modern Greek *turi pheta,* or "cheese slice." From the kindred Italian word for "slice," *fetta,* comes the term for the "sliced, ribbon-shaped" pasta called *fettucine.*

A *schnitzel* in German is a "little slice," a cousin of *schneiden,* "to cut," as well as *Schneider,* a surname that means "tailor." Similarly, the fish word *scrod* most likely derives from the obsolete Dutch word *schrood,* meaning "slice" or "shred." In English, *scrod* now applies to young fishes once they're prepared for cooking, particularly cod and haddock.

From the Old French *hacher,* "to chop up"—a linguistic relative of *hatchet*—comes the word *hash.* A *salpicon,* meanwhile, is another "chopped" word: the name of this thick sauce filled with chopped ingredients comes via French from the Spanish *salpicón,* from the Spanish *sal,* or "salt," and *picar,* which means "to chop," "to prick," or "to mince." The creamy East Indian mixture of lentils, onions, and spices called *dahl* or

∂al takes its name from the Hindi name for a type of pea, *∂āl,* which in turn comes from the Sanskrit *∂alati,* "he splits," because such legumes are split and dried for storage.

The sound of breaking may be audible inside the word *can∂y.* It's from the French *sucre candi,* or "candy sugar," which some scholars trace back to the Sanskrit *khan∂a,* meaning "sugar in pieces," from *khan∂,* meaning "to break."

Foods that are "pierced" include the thin, spicy fish slices called *sashimi,* which comes from the Japanese *sashi,* "stabbing," and *mi,* "body." *Shish kebab* arrived in this language via Armenian from a pair of Turkish words that mean "skewer" and "roast meat." Similarly, *steak* takes its name from the fact that such cuts of meat were once pierced and roasted on a spit. The word *steak* belongs to a large and "pointed" linguistic family that includes *stick, stigma, stitch,* and *instigate* (literally, "to prick" or "to prod" on). These words are also kin to the lively term *snickersnee,* which means either a "swordlike knife" or a "knife fight," from the Dutch phrase *steken of snijden,* "to stab or cut."

Some foods are named for the fact that they take a pounding. *Pesto* is one of them. Its name derives from the Italian for "pounded," making *pesto* a relative of such words as *piston* and *pestle. Couscous,* or in Arabic, *kuskus,* the North African pasta made from crushed, steamed semolina, gets its name from the Arabic *kaskasa,* a pounding-sounding word for "to pulverize." From the same source comes *cush,* the name of a cornmeal pancake brought to this country by African slaves and still popular in the southern United States.

From an Arabic word meaning "to grind" comes the name of the tasty paste of ground sesame seeds, *tahini.* Likewise, the powdery *meal* in such words as *cornmeal* belongs to a large linguistic family involving the notion of "grinding," which includes *molar, miller, malleable, mallet,* and *millet.* (The other sense of *meal,* as in breakfast, lunch, and dinner, comes from an ancient word for "measure" and is also seen in such words as *piecemeal.*)

Other edibles have names reflecting the fact that they're kneaded, massaged, or pressed. The soft, light yeast roll called a *brioche,* for example, comes from the Old French *broyer,* meaning simply "to knead." Another food with a "kneady" name is the Hawaiian dish *lomilomi.* This combination of chopped salmon, tomatoes, onions, and scallions is mixed by squeezing it through the fingers, which inspired its name, a native word that means "massage." And coffee brewed by forcing steam through finely ground, dark-roasted, powdered beans — that is, coffee that's literally "pressed out"—has a name that says so: *espresso.*

Foods that are literally "rolled" include *roulades, rollmops,* and, of course, *rolls. Roulades* usually consist of a slice of meat rolled around a filling. *Rollmops,* meanwhile, are hors d'oeuvres of pickled herring that take their name from the German *rollen,* "to roll" and *Mops,* meaning "pug dog," a reference to their stubby shape. Other foods' names indicate merely that they're "shaped" in some fashion, such as the French *fromage* and Italian *formaggio,* both of which mean "cheese" and are thought to stem from a Latin root reconstructed as "formed," *formāticus.*[1]

Foods That Are Mixed or Stuffed

Other foods are named for what's mixed into them. Originally mustard was made by mixing its aromatic ground seeds with new wine, or *must,* and the tubular pasta *mostaccioli* has a name that derives from the Latin *mustāceum,* "cake made with must." From the Latin for "seasoned with myrtle berries," or *murtatum,* comes the name of the sausage that traditionally contains such seasoning, *mortadella.* And *Wurst,* as in *liver-* and *brat-,* has a name reflecting the fact that these meat dishes are "mixed" with various seasonings: *Wurst* derives from an ancient root meaning "to confuse" or "to mix up" and is therefore a relative of *war,* which is characterized by extreme "confusion and discord."

From the Spanish *en,* "in," and *chile,* for "chili pepper," comes the word for a cheese-topped soft corn tortilla filled with seasoning containing chilies, *enchilada.*

---

[1] Incidentally, the French expression *faire des fromages,* literally, "to make cheeses," was borrowed and translated into English, where, as the *Oxford English Dictionary* helpfully explains, the phrase *to make cheeses* came to mean "a school-girl's amusement, consisting in turning rapidly round and then suddenly sinking down, so that the petticoats are inflated all round somewhat in the form of a cheese."

Foods that are stuffed or filled include *dolmas*, the Greek specialty of grape leaves stuffed with ground meat, herbs, or rice; their name derives from the Turkish *dolmak*, "to fill." Similarly, *gefilte fish*, those molded mixtures of ground fish, eggs, and spices, have a name that in Yiddish means "filled" or "stuffed" because originally the mixture was stuffed back into the fish skin before cooking. *Forcemeat*, the highly spiced, finely chopped meat dish, derives its name from the Latin *farcire*, "to stuff." *Forcemeat* and *farcire* are the etymological kin of *farce*, which originally denoted a brief, light-hearted play "stuffed in between" more weighty religious productions during the Middle Ages in the hope of keeping an audience from getting bored.

Foods That Come with Cooking Instructions

Several foods come with explicit linguistic instructions on how they should be prepared. *Zwieback*, the hard, sweet bread often given to teething infants, is an adaptation of the German *zwie*, "twice," and *backen*, "to bake." Similarly, back when *biscuits* had to last for months without refrigeration, they were baked, allowed to cool, then baked again—a cooking technique reflected in their name. *Biscuit* is a descendant of the Latin for "twice-cooked bread," *biscoctum pānem*. The *pānem*, or "bread," in this expression is a close relative of such words as *pantry*, a place where bread is stored.

And the *bis-* in *biscuit* is related to several other words involving "twos," including *bicycle* and *bicentennial,* while the *-cuit* in this "twice-cooked" food's name comes from the Latin *coquere,* meaning "to cook," the source also of *concoct, cuisine,* and *kitchen.* From the same Latin source comes the "twice-cooked" Italian cookies called *biscotti,* as well as *ricotta,* a cheese whose name means "cooked again." Still another edible etymological relative is *apricot,* from the Latin *praecoquere,* literally "to cook or ripen before," a reference to the apricot's tendency to ripen early in the year. The same Latin word also yielded our word describing a child who develops faster than others: *precocious.*

The name of the fish stew *bouillabaisse* tells exactly how to cook it. *Bouillabaisse* is adapted from the Provençal *bouiabaisso,* a word formed from the imperatives of verbs meaning "to boil" and "to lower"—a reference to the way in which it should be cooked by boiling, then immediately lowering the heat. The *-abaisse* in its name is analagous to the English *abase,* while the *bouill-* is related to the English *boil,* as well as to the thin broth made by simmering, *bouillon.* Meanwhile, the Dutch *zootje,* or "boiling," inspired the name of a once-popular dish of boiled perch, *water-souchy,* the *zootje* and *-souchy* being the etymological kin of the English *seethe.*

The thin-sliced Italian ham *prosciutto* takes its name from the Latin for "thoroughly sucked out"—an allusion to the fact that this thin-sliced meat is dry-cured—making *prosciutto* a relative of such words as *suck, suction,* and *succulent* (from the Latin *succus*, meaning "juice"). Foods that are "preserved" include *preserves*, of course, but also *pastrami*, the name of which is adapted via Yiddish from the Romanian *păstra*, "to preserve."

Melted foods include cheesy *fondue* and the creamy sugar paste known as *fondant*, both related to the name of the place where metal is melted, a *foundry*. "Parched" foods include *toast* and *tostada*, both of which stem from an ancient root meaning "to dry," the source also of *thirst, torrid*, and the Latin expression for "firm, dry land," *terra firma*.[2] (Incidentally, during the Middle Ages, European traders apparently applied the Latin name *terra merita*, or "meritorious earth," to an East Indian spice. Why they chose that name isn't clear, although they may have been trying to alter some native name for the spice into something more familiar to European ears. Whatever the reason, the name found its way into French as *terre mérite* and later into English as *turmeric*.)

The *pone* in *corn pone* explains how these hot cornmeal cakes should be prepared, for *pone* comes from an Algonquian word meaning "to roast" or "to bake." Some scholars believe that the *pita* in *pita bread* comes from a

---

[2] Surprisingly enough, another relative of these "dry, parched" words, is *torrent*, a descendant of the Latin *torrēre*, "to scorch, burn." A form of this word, *torrentem*, originally meant "burning" or "boiling." Gradually, however, it acquired the sense of "rushing" and "impetuous," so that the English descendant of this exceedingly "dry" root now means, ironically, a "rush of water."

Greek word for "cooked," *peptos*, a relative of several other "cooking" and "digestive" words, including *peptic* and *dyspepsia*.

Foods whose names are "fried" include the Chinese-American dish of stewed meat and veggies on fried noodles, *chow mein*, from the Mandarin Chinese *chǎo miàn*, or "to stir-fry noodles." The name of the small batter cakes called *fritters* arose from the Latin *frīgere*, "to fry." (*To fritter away*, however, contains an entirely different image. This type of *fritter* is thought to stem from the obsolete English word *fitters*, once a common term for "fragments," "pieces," or "atoms," which figured in the obsolete phrases "to tear to fitters" and "to be in fitters." Thus *to fritter away* means not "to fry" but "to tear away at something piece by piece," whether it's one's time, one's savings, or something else.) Also from the Latin *frīgere* come the English words *fry* and *fricassee*, a dish of chopped meat and vegetables, usually sautéed in butter and then stewed.[3]

Then there are all the *yaki*s, the Japanese word *yaki* meaning "to grill" or "to broil," as in *teriyaki* (literally, "glaze broil"), *sukiyaki* ("slice broil"), and *yakitori* ("broil fowl").

---

[3] The Greek name of a type of fricassee is thought to be the longest word ever to appear in all of literature: coined by the ancient playwright Aristophanes, the word is *lopadotemachoselachogaleokranioleipsanodrimhypotrimmatosilphiokarabomelitokatakechymenokichlepikossyphophattoperisteralektryonoptokephalliokigklopeleiolagoiosiraiobaphetraganopterygon*. Suffice it to say it's a fricassee that contains lots of ingredients.

Foods Named for Their Containers

Several food names contain the names of their containers. *Casserole*—a diminutive of the Old French *casse*, meaning "ladle" or "pan"—was first imported into English as a word denoting a kind of "stewpan." Only later did *casserole* come to specify that pan's contents. Like *casserole*, the French word *cassoulet* also originally denoted a kind of "stove dish" in French and only later came to designate the French-style mixture of white beans, meats, and vegetables it traditionally contains.

Then there's the French word for "stewpot," *chaudière*, which gave rise to the English word *chowder*. Both *chaudière* and *chowder* bubbled up from the Latin *calidus*, meaning "warm," as did at least two other food names: One is *caudle*, a warm drink of sweetened gruel mixed with wine or ale that women once sipped to soothe the pains of childbirth. Another is *chaudfroid*, a dish of cooked meat or fish served in a cold aspic or jelly, which, appropriately enough, literally means "hot-cold" in French. (Another close relative of all these "warm" words is *nonchalant*, a word that describes someone "not warm"—someone who is, in other words, "cool.")

Foods from pans include *pancakes*, of course, but also the saffron-flavored Spanish dish *paella*, whose name literally means "frying pan"; *paella* is a Spanish descendant of the Latin *patella*, or "little pan." (Roman physicians also applied the name *patella* to the flat bone in one's knee, a name that modern anatomists prefer over its less formal synonyms, *kneecap* and *kneepan.*) All these "pan" or "platter" words share a common ancestor with *paten,* the plate used in Christian religious services, and the *patina* that forms on copper surfaces, such as the copper plates and dishes used in antiquity.

Actually, many other words have evolved in this way, their meaning shifting from something that "contains" to what's contained inside it. The word *cash* is a case in point: originally this word specified a "chest or box for keeping money"; only later did *cash* come to apply to the contents of such a box. (*Cash,* incidentally, derives from the Latin word *capsa,* which designates a "box" or "coffer" and gives us the word *capsule. Capsa* is also thought to be related to the name of a pepper plant distinguished by its "boxy" podlike fruit, *capsicum.* Other derivatives of *capsa* include the English "container" word *case,* as well as *cassata,* a Neapolitan ice cream filled with candied fruit and nuts, which is molded into an oblong shape that resembles a "little case.")

A final example of a container contained in a food name is *lasagna.* This word's origin, however, is less than appetizing: in ancient Greece, a *lasanon* was a "chamber pot" or, as one Greek lexicon puts it, a "night chair." The Romans picked up on this word and later jokingly applied their version of it to a large cooking pot, calling it a *lasanum.* Eventually *lasanum* gave way to the modern Italian name for the hearty dish of flat noodles and sauce.

Foods Named for When and How They're Eaten

Other culinary names suggest when and how a food is eaten. *Lobster thermidor* is a case in point. Culinary legend holds that Napoleon first tasted this dish of creamed lobster meat and cheese during *Thermidor,* the eleventh month of the calendar devised during the French Revolution. The name *Thermidor,* specifying the period between July 19 and August 17, comes from the Greek words *thermos,* meaning "heat" (as in *thermometer* and *hypothermia*), and *dōron,* or "gift" (a relative of *donate, endow,* the "good gift" that is *Eudora,* and the "God-given" *Theodore*). The month of Thermidor fell between those with names that mean "harvest" and "fruit," in a cycle that also included months with names that translate as "fog," "snow," "sleet," "rain," "seed," "blossom," and, not surprisingly in this country of oenophiles, "vintage."

The name *endive* may reflect the season in which such plants are harvested. This name comes from the Medieval Greek *entubia,* thought by some etymologists to have come from the Egyptian word for "January," *tybi*—January being the month in which these plants were traditionally harvested. Similarly, because vegetables are planted in the spring, the Polish word for "springtime," *jarz,* is contained in that language's word for "vegetable," *jarzyna. Spring rolls,* on the other hand, are traditionally eaten in China and Southeast Asia during New Year's celebrations, which, as it happens, occur in the spring.

Another food whose name suggests timing is the *sundae*. One popular explanation for this name holds that, in order to skirt blue laws, which prohibited the sale of sinful soda pop on the Christian Sabbath at the turn of the twentieth century, enterprising soda-fountain owners invented this dessert as a kind of "ice cream soda"— without the soda water. Another version goes that the name simply refers to the fact that the extravagant addition of chocolate syrup made this cold treat far too expensive to eat except once a week, on Sundays.

Other foods are named for how they're eaten. *Chutney*, for example, comes from the Hindi word *catnī*, "to be licked" or "to be tasted," an apt name for this pungent relish. *Mangetout beans*, a kind of snow pea, have a name that in French means "eat all," a reference to the fact that both their peas and pods are edible.

Finally, some names simply reflect the fact that a food is eaten at all. The linguistic roots of *yam*, for example, lie in a West African term that was borrowed into Portuguese and Creole as *nyam*, or "to eat." Similarly, the frilly endive *escarole* derives from the Latin *ēsca*, which means, simply, "food." The Latin term derives from *edere*, "to eat," the source of *edible, eat, comestible*, and *etching*, the last of these being an image made when acid is used to "eat" away the surface of a metal plate. Oddly and unappetizingly enough, all these "eating" words are also closely related to the medical term *comedo*, which denotes the type of pustule also called a *whitehead*. (The surprising reason appears in Chapter 6.)

Foods Named for What They Do While Cooking

Bubble and squeak does just that, of course, while this potato-and-cabbage dish is greasily frying. The same is true for *singing hinny,* a griddle-baked spice cake that supposedly "sings" while cooking. (The *hinny* in its name is a northern England dialect term for *honey,* as in one's sweetheart.) *Bangers,* the British sausages, are so named because if they're not pricked before cooking, they'll explode like a firecracker—which in England is called a *banger.* And in Japan, the dipping broth called *shabu-shabu* has the sound of simmering in its name.

Other foods are named for the shapes they assume while cooking. In French, a *soufflé* is literally "puffed up," the linguistic product of the Latin for "to blow under." (*Soufflé,* in fact, is related to several other "blowing" words, including *flatulence* and *inflate,* as well as *flavor,* a word that originally meant "aroma" and only later acquired the meaning of "taste.") A *sad cake,* in contrast, sags in the middle while baking. *Crumpets* are so named because the original version of these griddle-baked breads tended "to curl up," an action denoted by the Middle English word *crumpen.*

The name of the Chinese wontons known as *pot stickers* contain a warning about what they'll do when frying if the cook's not careful: stick to the pot. And the *filé* in *filé gumbo* refers to the way the sassafras-based thickening agent known as *filé powder* forms long strands when added to hot liquid. From the French *filer,* "to spin," *filé* is kin to other "stringy" words, including *filigree* and the verb *to file* — originally, "to string things on a thread."[4] Sassafras, incidentally, is yet another food named for what it "does." Its name comes from the Latin *herba saxifragia,* literally a "rock-breaking plant," because it's often found growing in rock crevices. The *-fragia* and *-fras* in *saxifragia* and *sassafras* are kin to such "breaking" words as *fracture, fragment,* and *fragile.*

Another food named for what it supposedly "does" when cooked is *vol-au-vent,* a small puff-pastry shell stuffed with a ragout. The great French chef Marie-Antoine Carême claimed credit for its creation, boasting that when he took it from the oven, this dish was so light and airy that it "flew away in the wind." The *vol* in this flying food's name is a relative of the airborne words *volatile* and *volley,* while the *vent,* or "wind," in its name is related to *window, vent,* and *ventilate.* The same family of "windy" words produced the Sanskrit term for "blowing out" or "extinction" and, by extension, the blowing-out of individual existence and absorption into the supreme spirit, *nirvana.*

---

[4] *Gumbo* itself is African in origin, from a Bantu word for "okra." The colorful Creole phrase *gumbo ya-ya,* by the way, means either a "confused mess" or a "group of women talking excitedly together."

Foods Named for What They Do When Served

Sometimes a food's name derives from what it does when served—or what it's fancifully supposed to do. *Saltimbocca* is a contraction of the Italian *salta in bocca,* or "it leaps into the mouth," suggesting that a mouthful of this veal, spiced ham, and cheese dish is so tasty, it can't help but jump into one's mouth. The source of this name, the Latin *saltāre,* "to leap or jump," appears in two other food words: in French, *sauté* literally means "jumped"—a reference to the occasional tossing of a hot pan's contents—while the name *salmon* reflects this fish's well-known tendency to leap from the water. *Saltimbocca, sauté,* and *salmon,* incidentally, are relatives of several other words containing images of leaping. These include *salacious,* or "fond of leaping [onto something]" and therefore "lustful," as well as *desultory,* which means "leaping" and therefore "haphazard," and *salient,* which describes something that "leaps out" at an observer. The *bocca,* or "mouth," in *saltimbocca,* meanwhile, is related to the French *bouche,* or "mouth," and its Spanish counterpart, *boca,* as in the Florida city on an inlet shaped like a "rat's mouth," *Boca Raton.* The word *collop,* meaning "slice of meat," may contain the faint outlines of another saltatory image. Although its etymology is obscure, many scholars think *collop* evolved from the Swedish term for "meat stew," *kalops,* which in turn arose from the Old Swedish *kolhuppadher,* meaning "something that hops on coals."

The Mexican dish *manchamanteles* contains an equally colorful description of what happens once it's served. This stew of pork, chicken, almonds, tomatoes, pineapple, plantain, spices, and jicama has a cautionary name: *manchamanteles* means "it stains tablecloths"—a reference to its red sauce. Yet another food named for what it "does" when served is the Japanese shrimp dish *odori*, which means "dancing"—because the creatures are eaten alive and wriggle their last when dipped into a spicy sauce.

Other foods are named for what supposedly happens when they're eaten. A *ragout*, for example, is literally supposed to "revive the taste." *Ragout* is a descendant, via French, of the Latin *gustus*, or "taste," the source of *gusto* and *disgust*, or "extreme distaste." (The thick Kentucky stew called *burgoo*, incidentally, is thought to be an alteration of *ragout*.) Also invigorating: a *ravigote*, the piquant vinegar sauce that takes its name from the French *ravigoter*, "to add new vigor," and is closely related to *vigor* and *vegetable*, the latter of which comes from the Latin *vegēre*, "to be lively,"

An even perkier mouthful is *tiramisù*, the rich dessert of rum and buttery mascarpone cheese, whose name translates from an Italian dialect as "pick me up." Livelier still is the name of the hot chili pepper that some East Africans call *pili-pili ho-ho*, or "chili that makes you say 'ho-ho.' "

Spaniards, meanwhile, sup on a dish of cod with the baffling name *atascaburras*, which conjures a grisly image—"it chokes the female burro"—not to be confused with the ropy Italian pasta *strozzapreti,* whose name means "it strangles priests." In Andalusia, the fried-fish preparation known as *bienmesabe* has a much kinder reputation for pleasing; its name means simply "it tastes good to me." And in Portugal, the almond sweet called *comer e chorar por mais* goes by an especially optimistic name that means "eat and cry for more."

Finally, there's *aubergine,* a French name for the egg-plant, which gives a clue to this food's after-dinner effects. Traced back to the Arabic *al-bādinjān,* an adaptation of the Persian *bādingān, aubergine* derives ultimately from this plant's Sanskrit name, *vatingana,* a relative of all those "windy" words such as *nirvana.* In Sanskrit, *vatingana* apparently means an "antifart vegetable" or, as the *Oxford English Dictionary* notes, the type of vegetable that "removes the . . . windy humor."

6

FOOD
FOR
THOUGHT

*Words Deriving from Other Words
About Food and Drink*

℘oet and literary critic Owen Barfield once observed that, just as coal and wine yield up their bottled sunshine when kindled or sipped, so too can
words be "made to disgorge the past that is bottled
up inside of them." Whenever etymologists pry
open a word and coax out its secrets, the results are
illuminating indeed. A word's history often sheds

new light upon the ways in which our predecessors tried to make sense of the world. Like a poem, a single word can record a moment of inspired creativity, one in which our ancestors perceived a similarity between two seemingly unrelated ideas and joined them to form another that was wholly new. As the writer Thomas Carlyle put it in 1843, "The coldest word was once a glowing new metaphor."

Who would have thought, for example, that inside the name of the fabric *seersucker* lie words for two different kinds of foods? Who'd have imagined that inside the word *lady* is the image of a loaf of bread? Or that the delicious word *mellifluous* is literally flowing with honey?

Pablum, flummery, castanets, credenza, high muckety-muck, galaxy, sycophant — all contain vivid images of food and drink, eating and imbibing. With the words that follow, we'll brush off the dust from a number of linguistic fossils to uncover the surprising images within.

alma mater The tender image of a "nourishing mother" appears in this fond Latin term for one's academic institution. From the Latin *alere*, "to nourish," also comes *alimentary*, as well as the name for those who have received intellectual sustenance, *alumni*. (Some of those alums will no doubt wind up supplying a different — but etymologically related — kind of support to their former college sweethearts in the form of *alimony*.)

The *mater*, or "mother," in *alma mater* is a relative of such words as *maternal, matrimony, matrix* (originally, a "breeding animal" and later the "situation in which something originates or develops"), and *matriculate* (originally to become part of a matrix and later "to register" to be part of a college or university). *Mater* is also kin to the Greek word for "mother city," *metropolis.*

bagatelle This word for any "slight or insignificant thing" was plucked from an Italian word that comes from the Latin for "berry," *baca.* Both *bagatelle* and *baca* are the linguistic kin of *Bacchus,* the grape-loving Roman god who would probably appreciate the fact that the word *bagatelle* now applies to any light, festive composition in music or verse. Also from *baca* comes another name for the laurel tree, *bay tree.* The bay, which bears small, dark berries, is the source of the subtly aromatic spice *bay leaves.*

botulism Because it was first identified in people who had suffered the misfortune of eating bad sausage, the name for this dangerous form of food poisoning comes from the Latin word for "sausage," *botulus.* The diminutive of *botulus* is *botellus,* which became the Latin word for not only a "small sausage," but the "small intestine" that encases sausage. The sausage word *botellus* eventually wound up, as it were, in the English word *bowels. Botellus* apparently also gave rise to the Old French word for "sausage," *boudin,* which in turn led to the English word *pudding,* which was first applied to sausages. Later the word *pudding* expanded to indicate any of several dishes boiled or steamed in a sausage-shaped bag or cloth and eventually came to designate a variety of soft foods.

bubkes, bupkes This expressive Yiddish word for something trifling or outrageously insignificant (as in "I work my fingers to the bone and what do they pay me? *Bubkes!*") is an etymological relative of the Russian for "small beans" and the Yiddish for "goat turd."

buccaneer Seventeenth-century French explorers who hunted the plentiful wild boars and oxen on Caribbean islands enthusiastically adopted the native custom of barbecuing the meat and drying it on a rack called a *bocan*. This local word for "barbecue frame" gave rise to the French verb *boucaner*, "to dry or smoke meat," and a practitioner of this technique came to be known as a *boucanier*. When the explorers weren't having cookouts, they plundered Spanish ships passing through the area and eventually became known as *buccaneers*.

butterfly Embarrassingly enough for this lovely insect, an old Dutch word for this creature, *boterschijte*, means "butter shit." Many etymologists (not to mention entomologists) suspect that the name of this insect refers to the color of its droppings. Another hypothesis, however, is that the *butter* refers to the fact that in some European countries butterflies traditionally were regarded as witches or fairies who filch milk and butter and then fly off with it—hence this insect's German name, *Milchdieb,* or "milk thief."

Whatever the source of this name, it's worth noting that the *butter* in *butterfly* comes from a Greek word meaning "cow cheese." The Greek *boutyron* (and therefore the English *butter*) belong to a whole herd of *bovine* words, including *bovine* and *bulimia*—literally, "ox hunger"—as well as *bucolic* and *bugle,* which comes from the Latin for "little ox" and originally applied to a type of ox horn used as both a drinking vessel and a musical instrument. Another linguistic relative is the name of a method of writing used in some ancient Mediterranean cultures, including some predecessors of the ancient Greeks, *boustrophedon.* Pronounced "boo-struh-FEED-un," this term denotes a system in which one line is inscribed with the letters proceeding from right to left, the next from left to right, and the next from right to left again. Its name, which literally means "turning like an ox," refers to the fact that the reader's eye follows a path similar to that of an ox plowing a field. This word herd also includes *beef,* the French *bœuf,* and the family name that literally means "cowherd," *Bouvier.*

careen At the turn of the seventeenth century, *careen* meant "to turn a ship over on its side for cleaning or repairs." Later this word's meaning expanded to indicate the lurching, swerving motion of a ship, and later still, *careen* came to apply to the action of anything that rushes headlong. This word's roots, however, are in the Latin word *carīna,* which means both "keel" and "nutshell" and is related to the Sanskrit *karaka-* "coconut." (In the same way, a French word for "nutshell," *chaloppe,* inspired the English name for the type of boat called a *shallop.* Both *chaloppe* and *shallop* are linguistic cousins of the boat-shaped Tex-Mex culinary creation that carries a cargo of savory ingredients, the *chalupa.*)

Speaking of nuts, the precursor of the modern English *in a nutshell* apparently dates back to antiquity. It's said that the Roman orator Cicero, who as we saw in Chapter 4 was himself named after a food, once alluded to a parchment copy of the *Iliad* that supposedly was written in such small script that the whole thing literally fit into a nutshell. Now, this would be very fine print indeed, considering that this ancient epic of love, war, and valor contains a grand total of 501,930 letters. At any rate, throughout the eighteenth and nineteenth century, speakers of English showed off their erudition by describing anything similarly condensed as *an Iliad in a nutshell.* Later this phrase contracted into its present form, which usually denotes a brief summation of something lengthy.

castanet The seventeenth-century writer who described a group of dancers accompanying themselves with "knockers on their fingers" was referring to the clicking and clacking of *castanets*. Our word for these percussive instruments comes from the Latin for "chestnut," *castanea*. The English word *castaneous* is a perfectly useful, though little-used, synonym for "chestnut-colored."

Speaking of which, the claret hue of the large, sweet chestnut that the French call a *marron* inspired the word for the dark color we now call *maroon*.

(The verb *maroon*, however, as in *marooned on a desert island*, comes from an entirely different source: During the seventeenth and eighteenth centuries, some of the Africans who were kidnapped by white traders and taken to the West Indies managed to escape to the surrounding mountains. To the Spaniards, such a person was a *cimarrón*, a word meaning "wild" or "untamed," which may arise from the Spanish word *cima*, meaning "peak" or "mountaintop." The French shortened this to *marron*, and English speakers later used the term specifically to denote "a runaway slave." Thus in 1626 a writer mentioned "The Symerons (a blacke people, which about eightie yeeres past, fled from the Spaniards their Masters)." Forty years later, another writer noted in his history of the Caribbean that such slaves "run away and get into the Mountains and Forests, where they live like so many Beasts; then they are call'd Marons, that is to say Savages." Before long, *to be marooned* became an expression applied to anyone who's been left high and dry.

comedo Although the ancient Romans used this word to mean "a glutton"—it's a derivative of *edere*, "to eat," and a relative of such words as *edible*—*comedo* is used in English to mean something quite unappetizing. According to the *Oxford English Dictionary*, a *comedo* is "a small worm-like yellowish black-tipped pasty mass which can in some persons be made, by pressure, to exude from hair follicles. They are found on the cheeks, forehead, and nose." The *OED* goes on to explain that the Latin term *comedo*, meaning "glutton," later came to be applied to gluttonous maggots or "worms that devour the body." Later still, physicians applied the term *comedo* to the contents of a whitehead, which do after all resemble such a creature. As one 1874 homeopathic medical textbook helpfully explains, "This collection when squeezed out of the skin, is emitted in a cylindrical form, having the appearance of a small grub or maggot (*comedones*), hence it is sometimes called 'maggot-pimple' or 'whelk.' "

Strangely, another synonym for "whitehead," *milium*, is also a food word. The word was borrowed into English from Latin, where it meant "millet," and is now used to denote a "whitehead," due to the resemblance between the two.

companion From the Latin *com-*, meaning "with," and *-pānis*, "bread," comes this poetic term that literally means the "person with whom one shares bread." *Companion* is related to several other bread words, including *pantry*, the loaf-shaped cigar called a *panatela*, and *panniers*, those large wicker baskets that fit across the backs of pack animals.

Another synonym for "companion," *mate* also has its origins in eating together. It comes from the Middle Low German *māte* or *gemate*, meaning "messmate"—a person, in other words, with whom one regularly shares food.

confetti Italians eat *confetti* by the handful, *confetti* being their word for the sugar-coated almonds often handed out as party favors. Actually, this usage is closer to the true origins of the word: the Latin *cōnficere*, or "to make ready or put together," which also led to the English *confection* as well as *comfit*, a sweetmeat that features a solid center of a fruit, root, nut, or seed and that is "put together" with sugar. (A *discomfiting* remark, on the other hand, is a discombobulating comment that leaves one feeling most *un-put-together.*)

What English speakers call *confetti*, at any rate, the Italians call *coriandoli*, or "corianders." In their earliest form, these tiny, lemony-flavored comfits, which had a coriander seed at their core, were tossed at festive occasions, such as Carnivale. Later, *confetti* expanded to include tiny paper discs, as well as little balls of soft white plaster that left marks wherever they were thrown. (A synonym for the English *comfit*, by the way, is *sugar plum*. Sir Walter Scott once put the term to good use when describing a scene in which "compliments flew about like sugar-plums at an Italian carnival.")

crambo In the days before television, talk radio, and on-line chat, English folk amused themselves with the rhyming game *crambo*, in which one player had to come up with a line that rhymes with one from another player, but without using any words from the previous line. The name *crambo* comes from the Latin *crambē* (*repetīta*), which means "twice-cooked cabbage." The ancient Romans used this expression as a disparaging term for "dull or pedestrian writing." The Latin phrase echoes an earlier Greek proverb that goes *dis krambe thanatos*, or "cabbage twice over is death," a joking reference to the extreme distastefulness of boring, stale writing, or repetition.

In the nineteenth century, *dumb crambo* described a popular form of charades in which members of one team choose a word, then act out words that rhyme with it in an effort to help the others guess it. If, for example, the secret word is *cat*, the players might try to pantomime such words as *bat, hat, fat, splat, pat, rat,* and *sat.* (And if a couple of rounds of *dumb crambo* didn't result in a rip-roaring good time, they could always try their hands at other amusements named for food, such as a *Cheddar letter.* Popular in the seventeenth and eighteenth centuries, this game required each of several people to contribute one paragraph to a letter, in the hope that the result would somehow fit together in the same way that Cheddar cheese is made with contributions from several different dairies. Then there's *honeypots,* another past pastime with food in its name. According to *Webster's Third New International Dictionary,* it's "a game in which a child (called the *honeypot*) with his hands clasped under his hams is swung backward and forward by his arms until his grip relaxes in order to find his weight which is reckoned at a pound for each swing.")

credenza Considering the lack of refrigeration and abundance of royal enemies during the Middle Ages, the kings, queens, and other aristocrats who insisted that underlings taste every course of a meal before serving were probably more prudent than paranoid. Before a meal, servants would spread out all its courses along a low side table, known in English as a *credence,* in French as a *crédence,* and in Italian as a *credenza* — all from the Medieval Latin *credentia,* or "belief" — and proceed to establish the food's *credibility,* or "trustworthiness."

Although the English word for this rather macabre minibuffet became obsolete, the Italian version lives on in our word for any "low bookcase, table, or sideboard." *Credenza* belongs to a family of trusty words that include *credit, credible,* and *creed,* as well as the verb *grant,* which first meant "to agree to, allow, concede" and later came to mean "to bestow formally."

dope Around the turn of the nineteenth century, Americans borrowed and slightly altered the Dutch word *doop,* or "dipping sauce," applying it to various types of thick fluids. In those days, a *dope* could be anything from gravy to skin cream to pitch smeared on the bottom of shoes to help them move easily across half-melted snow. Even today, as Craig M. Carver's richly informative *A History of English in Its Own Words* points out, some Ohioans still ask a server to add "dope," or dessert topping, to their ice cream or pudding.

By the mid–nineteenth century, the word was also applied to anyone so dense he might as well have some sort of dope for brains. In the 1880s, its meaning extended even further, when *dope* became synonymous with the gummy preparation used in making opium. Those under the influence of opium—or whose sluggishness or stupidity made them seem that way—soon were described as being *dopey.*

doughnutting According to *The Oxford Dictionary of New Words*, the ringed shape of the doughnut inspired this Information Age term, which means "the clustering of politicians round a speaker during a televised parliamentary debate so as to fill the shot and make the speaker appear well-supported."

E pluribus unum Chosen as the motto for a newly united nation, the Latin phrase *E pluribus unum* means "from many, one." The expression first appeared, however, in an ancient Roman poem as part of a recipe for making a fresh garden salad.

festoon Adapted from the Italian *festone*, or "decoration for a feast," *festoon* first graced the English language in the late seventeenth century, where it denoted a smile-shaped garland of flowers or leaves, hung from two points and sagging slightly in the middle. It later became a verb that means "to adorn."

A visual echo of such decoration appears on *festonati*, tubes of Italian pasta stamped with garlandlike images along its sides. And speaking of feasting, the name of those graceful swoops that once adorned dining halls is now also a term in modern dentistry, where the word *festoon* denotes "the garlandlike area of the gums surrounding the necks of the teeth."

flummery This term for meaningless chatter or deceptive language is one of several similarly disparaging words deriving from foods. This particular one comes from the Welsh *llymru,* which is a kind of soft jelly made from sour oatmeal.

foster *Foster* is one of many common English words that arose from a prehistoric root meaning "to protect" or "to feed." These include several words of Germanic origin, such as *feed, food,* and *fodder,* as well as the feeding words that found their way into English through the Romance languages, including *pasture, pastoral, repast,* and *companion,* or "bread sharer."

A similar connection between the notion of *fostering* and *feeding* occurs in French. There *nourricière* means "nutritious" and a foster mother is a *mère nourricière,* while a foster child is a *nourrisson.* (Both *nutritious* and *nourricière,* as well as *nourrisson* and *nutrient,* are the etymological offspring of the Latin *nūtrīre,* "to nourish," the source also of the term for the most fundamental means of nourishing, *nursing.*)

This notion of defining close relationships based on shared sustenance is also evident in the French for "foster sister," *sœur de lait.* Literally, such a person is a "sister of milk," while a "foster brother" is a *frère de lait.* The same idea is reflected in the little-used English term *milk brother,* which also means "foster brother"—as does its equiva-

158

lent in several other languages, including the German *Milchbruder,* Russian *molochnyi brat,* and Serbian *mlenci brat.* (An English term for a half sibling, *even-sucker,* also alludes to milk. The word *even,* in this case, means "fellow" or "co-"; the use of *sucker,* meanwhile, arose from a time when nursing infants were indeed called just that.)

Yet another term that suggests "we are with whom we eat" is the English expression *cater-cousin.* A descendant of the English *cater*—which originally meant the person who bought *cates,* or "provisions," for a household—*cater-cousin* applied in the sixteenth century to people who technically weren't first cousins but were still closely related by a distant family connection, or by intimate friendship or some other common interest. Shakespeare, for example, alludes to a pair of *cater-cousins* in *The Merchant of Venice.* This term apparently arose from the notion that such intimates were as close as if they had been *catered,* or "boarded," together—that, in other words, they literally had been companions for some times.

galaxy The Greek astronomer Ptolemy referred to the swath of stars that cuts across the nighttime sky as the *galaktikos kyklos,* or the "milky circle." The *kyklos* is an ancestor of the English *cycle,* and the *galaktikos* comes from the Greek *gala,* or "milk," the source of the modern English *galaxy.* The Romans called this cloudy collection of stars the *via lactea*, or "milky way," *lactea* deriving from the Latin for "milk," *lac*, the source also of the English *lactate* and *lactic acid*. *Lac* also produced the English *lettuce*, a vegetable so called because, when cut, some varieties exude a milky juice. (This etymological connection is even clearer in the words for "lettuce" and "milk" in French, *laitue* and *lait*, as in *café au.*) The Latin word for "milk" flavors words in other languages as well, including the Spanish *leche* and the breast-feeding enthusiasts known as the *La Leche League*. *Lac* also put the milk into the Italian coffee drink known as *latte*.

The Romans, incidentally, said that the Milky Way had spurted from Juno's breasts and that the drops that had fallen to earth had turned into lilies. English poets of the sixteenth and seventeenth centuries used the term *milky way* to refer to "the region of a woman's breasts," as in "Two snowy mounts, so near her heart. . . . Between those hills, a milky way there leads" and "Behold her heav'nly face and heaving milky way."

garble Although today *to garble* usually means to turn something into a confused mess, originally this verb referred to a process of separating out and making neater. Specifically, it meant to sift out the usable parts of herbs and spices from those to be thrown away. *Garble* is from the Italian *garbellare*, itself a product of the Arabic *gharbala*, "to sift" or "to select." Describing an Alexandrian marketplace in 1599, one writer observed, "All sortes of spices be garbled after the bargaine is made." A half century later, another writer used the word in a description of the occupational hazards of doing such work with red peppers: "We fall all a Coughing, which lasts . . . as long as we are garbling it."

The refuse removed from such spices was known as the *garble,* and the official responsible for garbling the garble and making sure that such transactions were conducted fairly was called the *garbler.*

Garble's Arabic ancestor, *gharbala,* by the way, is apparently a derivative of the Latin word *cribellare,* "to sift." (From the same source also comes the modern Spanish verb *garbilliare,* "to sift corn.") This would make *garble* a relative of other "sifting out and deciding" words, including *discern* and *certain.* It's also a cousin of the Old English *briddle,* meaning "sieve," the source of the verb *to riddle,* as in "to shoot full of holes." (The *riddle* that is a puzzle, however, arose from an entirely different root meaning "to fit together," which produced several other linguistic offspring that involve some sort of "fitting together," such as *read* and *reason.*)

ginkgo Distinguished by its yellow, wedge-shaped leaves and extraordinarily smelly fruits, this ancient tree gets its name from the Japanese *ginkyo*, which in turn derives from the Chinese expression *yinhsing*, or "silver apricot."

grenade The shape of this incendiary device inspired its name, which is a direct borrowing of the French word for "pomegranate." (In the U.S. military, a *grenade* is jokingly called a *pineapple* because of its shape.) Both the French *grenade* and the English *pomegranate* come from the Old French *pome grenate*, "an apple with many seeds or 'grains.' "[1] This fruit's French name also yielded that of the thick, sweet red syrup made from pomegranates, *grenadine*. The deep red color of the fruit's seeds may also have inspired the name of the gemstone *garnet*.

Incidentally, the vaselike shape of the wild pomegranate's blossoms inspired two other familiar terms. It seems the ancient Greeks' name for this blossom, *balaustion*, led to the English words *baluster*—a vase-shaped support for a handrail on a staircase—and *balustrade*, which refers to both the rail and balusters together. Over the centuries, *baluster* became *barrester*, eventually evolving into

---

[1] The *-granate* in *pomegranate*, in turn, comes from a family of "granular" words that include *corn*, *kernel*, and *grain*. A misreading of the Old French word for a "many-seeded stew or sauce," *grane*, may have led to the Middle English word *grave*, the predecessor of the modern English *gravy*.

the word now used to denote the type of handrail known as a *banister.*

gridiron In Middle English, a *gridel* was the set of parallel metal bars upon which foods were placed for broiling. This word is a descendant of the Latin *craticula,* or "little lattice" (also the source of the English *grill*). Under the influence of the Middle English *iren,* or "iron," *gridel* evolved into the name of the culinary tool called a *gridiron.* This cooking device in turn bequeathed its name to the football field that resembles it.

From *gridiron* also comes *griddle,* plus the pattern of intersecting lines called a *grid* — as well as the nerve-racking results of heavy traffic gumming up a grid of streets, *gridlock.* A grisly footnote, however: the earliest recorded uses of both *gridiron* and *griddle* were in thirteenth-century England, when both words referred to an instrument of torture on which its victims were literally roasted.

groggy British admiral Sir Edward Vernon, who won military renown during the memorably named War of Jenkins' Ear in 1739, was known for wearing a favorite coat made of *grogram.* The name of this stiff material is an alteration of the French *gros grain,* or "coarse texture," from *gros,* meaning "coarse" or "thick" (a relative of the English *gross*), and *graine,* meaning "grain" or "seed." This trademark attire earned the commander the nickname *Old Grog.* Admiral Vernon was also a notoriously harsh disciplinarian, a reputation confirmed by his order to dilute his thirsty crew's ration of rum with water in order to cut costs. Grumbling sailors named the miserably weak drink after him, calling it *grog*.

As later happened with the word *dope*, the name of this intoxicating substance led to an adjective describing someone who is under its influence, or at least acts *groggy*. It also inspired the picturesque term *grog blossom* for that reddening of the schnozz common to heavy drinkers. The nineteenth-century author Thomas Hardy put this term to colorful use when he observed of someone that "a few grog-blossoms marked the neighbourhood of his nose."

Despite Admiral Vernon's parsimonious ways, he did manage to win the undying loyalty of at least one subordinate, one Laurence Washington. Years later, when Washington's half brother George felt burdened by the pressures of the presidency, he would slip away to Laurence's peaceful Virginia estate, which, in honor of his beloved Old Grog, the navy veteran had christened *Mount Vernon*.

high muckety-muck This term comes from the language of the Chinooks, a Native American people of the Pacific Northwest. In Chinook slang, *hayo makamak* literally means "plenty to eat" or "much food" and applies to wealthy tribal members who can afford to eat well. English-speaking interlopers later misunderstood the term as *high muckamuck* or *high muckety-muck* and applied it to anyone important or influential—particularly someone conceited about it.

hodgepodge In Middle English, a "jumble" or "mixture of various ingredients" was sometimes called a *hochepot*. This term was borrowed whole from Old French, where *hochepot* was a culinary term for "stew," from *hochier*, "to shake together," and *pot*, meaning "pot." Even earlier, however, *hochepot* referred to the mixing together of property to ensure its equitable distribution, as among the heirs of someone who had died without a will. In modern English, this "shaking together of the pot" goes by the legal term *hotchpot*.

Several other food terms gave rise to words that now denote a "hodgepodge" or "mixture." One of these is the delicious word *gallimaufry*. This word may come from the Old French *galimafree*, meaning "sauce" or "ragout" (a combination of *galer*, "to make merry," and *mafrer*, "to gorge oneself").

Similarly, *farrago* comes from the Latin *farrāgō*, meaning "mixed fodder for cattle," and is related to *farina*, the bland, fine-ground cereal that takes its name from the Italian *farro*, or "spelt." *Salmagundi*, a word of obscure origin, once denoted a spicy stew of chopped meat, anchovies, eggs, onions, lemon juice, and oil. Later, however, *salmagundi*'s meaning was extended to any kind of "jumble of ingredients." ("His mind was a sort of salmagundi," one writer noted in 1797.) A few years later this word was popularized in the United States by the humorous periodical *Salmagundi, or The Whim-Whams and Opinions of Launcelot Langstaff, Esq. and Others.* Written by Washington Irving, his brother William, and a friend, the publication featured satirical essays on contemporary topics written under silly pseudonyms.

One last "mixed-up" food word: *pasticcio.* Now denoting a "musical or artistic composition made up of pieces from different sources," *pasticcio* is borrowed directly from Italian, where it indicates a pastry-enclosed jumble, a *pie.* In fact, in modern Italian, *fare un pasticcio* — literally "to make a pie" — also means "to make a dreadful mess of things."

junket These days a *junket* is a kind of pleasure trip, particularly one made by a government official at public expense. The source of *junket* is the Latin word *juncus,* or "reed." In early English, *junket* meant "basket made from reeds or rushes," and indeed an early translation of the Bible describes how Moses' mother put her baby into a *ionket of resshen,* or "junket of rushes," before setting it into the Nile.

Fifteenth-century Brits enjoyed a delicacy of sweetened, curdled milk that was set into a small reed basket or onto a woven mat to drain before serving. Like *lasagna* and other foods named for their containers, this creamy dessert took on the name of the basket, *junket*. A century later, the meaning of *junket* extended to various sweet cakes and other delicacies, as well as to revelries that involved food and drink, such as banquets or picnics. The always fun-loving and enterprising Americans picked up that idea and ran with it, and by the late 1800s they were using the term *junket* specifically to mean a jaunt for which others, particularly taxpayers, get stuck with the bill.

Speaking of reeds, the ancient Greeks called a reed a *kanna*, and a basket made from it was called a *kanastron*. From this Greek word, in turn, arose the Latin *canistrum*, meaning "a basket for bread, fruit, or flowers." Eventually this reedy word found its way into English as *canister*. From the same linguistic family comes the tube-shaped Italian pasta *cannelloni*, the English *cane*, and *cannellure* (a lengthwise groove on a column). They're also related to *canel*, an obsolete word that, like the modern French *cannelle* and Spanish *canela*, denotes a stick of the rolled, tubular bark we call cinnamon. (The word *cinnamon* itself, by the way, derives ultimately from a Semitic name for this spice.)

knapsack From the Low German *knappen*, which means "to make a loud snapping noise," "to bite into," or "to eat," comes a modern German word for "food," *Knapp*. *Knappen* also apparently inspired the name of a bag for carrying such provisions, *Knappsack,* which became anglicized as *knapsack.*

Other mordant, or "biting," words involving food and drink include *morsel* (literally a "bite" and a close relative of *mordant,* or "biting") and *schnapps,* that lip-smacking mouthful of liquor that derives its name from the Middle Low German *snappen,* "to snap at." These words are also related to the English *knap,* meaning "to bite abruptly" or "to snap." Although not used often nowadays, the word *knap* proved handy for Shakespeare, who has a character in *The Merchant of Venice* observe, "I would she were as lying a gossip in that as ever knapp'd ginger."

laetrile This controversial anticancer drug is made from a chemical called *amygdalin,* from the Latin *amygdala,* or "almond," a bitter-almond-flavored extract that comes from apricot and peach pits. Early anatomists also applied the name *amygdala* to a small almond-shaped structure inside the brain's temporal lobe.

Amygdalin, at any rate, is key to the manufacture of *laetrile,* the name of which is a shortening of *L-mandelonitrile,* the *mandel* inside it coming from the German word for "almond," *Mandel.* Speaking of which, in his great dictionary of 1755 Samuel Johnson notes that in English tonsils used to be called *almonds of the throat.*

lampoon In many French drinking songs, the most important part is the imperative in the refrain, "*Lampons!*," or "Let's drink!" It is this boozy exhortation, many etymologists believe, that inspired our word for "satire" or "ridicule." The French *lampons* and *lampoon* are thought to stem from a Germanic source. So does the English word involving merrymaking, *carouse*, which is an adaptation of German *gar aus*, or "all out," as in "time to leave the bar." This expression has evolved to mean "drink up" or "one last drink before closing time" and eventually to a whole evening's worth of "sitting around drinking until closing time."

lens The Latin word for "lentil," *lens*, inspired several words for items that are convex in shape, or *lenticular*. In French, the word *lentille* can mean either "lens" or "lentil"; its plural means "freckles." Similarly, in the sixteenth and seventeenth centuries, the English *lentil* also denoted both the "freckle" and the legume. Today, *lento* remains a glorified English word for "freckle," while someone who is heavily freckled is said to be *lentiginous*. Yet another word for "freckle" was inspired by the fact that these bits of pigment resemble "little fern seeds"—which means that writers who fret that they've used the word *lentiginous* too many times in one paragraph can always go back and substitute the handy synonym *ferniticled*.

lord In medieval England, the male head of a household called himself the "keeper of the bread," or *hláfweard,* (literally "loaf-ward"). The servants who depended on him to give them that day their daily bread were called *hláfáetan,* literally, "bread eaters." Over the years, *hláfweard* softened into *hláford,* with its *f* pronounced like a *v.* Later still, this word for the master of a house smoothed into *lord.*

A similar notion of boss-man-as-keeper-of-the-bread appears in the modern German words for "employer": *Brotgeber* ("bread giver") and *Brotherr* ("bread herr," no relation to the English *brother*). Another version of this idea is preserved within the terms long used to designate the lady of the house in Sweden, Denmark, and Iceland—*matmoder, maðmoder,* and *matmóðir*—names that literally translate as "meat mother."

The lord of the house may have owned the bread, but the member of the family who was stuck with the job of kneading the dough in the first place was the *hlǽfðige,* or "bread kneader"—a word eventually smoothed out by centuries of use into *lady.* The *-dy* in *lady* contains the remnants of an ancient root meaning "to shape or form," which also helped to form the Old English *dág,* a forerunner of the modern English *dough.* This notion of kneading is also in the Old English word *dǽge,* or "kneader," which went on to become *dey,* which originally meant "breadmaker." *Dey* later came to apply more generally to a "female servant" and sometimes also to a "milkmaid." In turn, the place where that particular type of a dey tended to the milk came to be known as a *dairy*.[2]

mange This skin disease induced by parasites takes its name from an Old French term meaning "eating" or "itch." It's related to several other "eating" words, including *manger*, a trough from which animals eat, and *blancmange*, the dessert whose name literally means "white edible."[3]

Mange is also kin to that most welcome of Italian invitations, *"Mangia!"* All of these words are also related to an obsolete English word worth reviving, *gramaungere*, which, like its Old French predecessor, *grant mangier*, means "a great meal."

mealy-mouthed Imagine talking while trying to hold a mouthful of flour or other fine-ground meal without spilling it, and it's immediately clear why

---

[2] The word *dough*, incidentally, may also be part of the word *dogie*, a term for a "motherless calf." Although this word's origin is not entirely clear, it may have arisen during some lean years in the American West, in which many starving, orphaned, swollen-bellied calves wandered the range. Likening their bellies to "a batch of sourdough carried in a sack," cowboys referred to such calves as *dough-guts*, a shortened form of which, *dogie*, survives in "Get along, little . . ."

[3] The name of another disease, *lupus erythematosus*, also involves eating; it's a borrowing of the Latin *lupus*, or "wolf," and is so called because of the wolflike voracity with which it attacks the skin.

mealy-mouthed is an apt description for someone who speaks evasively, equivocally, or not much at all. Etymologists suspect that English speakers adapted this term from a German phrase used by theologian Martin Luther. Never one to pass up an opportunity to denounce hypocrisy, Luther used the expression *Mehl im Maule behalten*—"to carry meal in the mouth"—to describe someone who was speaking in exactly that kind of equivocating manner.

The softness of fine-ground meal, incidentally, may have inspired the word *mellow,* while the ancient ritual of sprinkling a sacrifice with salted meal (or *mola salsa* in Latin) before igniting it led to the considerably less-than-mellow English word that now means "to kill with fire" or "to utterly destroy," *immolate.*

(Speaking of burnt sacrifices, by the way, the ancient Greeks' word *thuein,* "to burn sacrificially," inspired the name of a fragrant spice they often burned on such occasions. The faint outlines of this ancient word are now visible in this herb's modern English name, *thyme.*)

mellifluous The Latin words *mel,* "honey," and *fluere,* "to flow," combined to produce this word, which describes a dulcet-toned voice or anything else smooth and sweet. From the same Latin root come two more sweet words, *marmalade* and *molasses.*

172

The Latin *mel*'s Greek equivalent, *meli*, may be the source of the feminine name *Pamela*, which some etymologists think means "all honey." It's also in *Melissa*, which in Greek means "bee" and may stem from two Greek words that literally mean "honey licker." (The related Russian word for "bear," *medved*, literally means "honey eater.") Another member of this family of honeyed words is the Latin word *mulsus*, or "honey sweet," which apparently influenced the French name of the dessert now familiar to English palates as *mousse*.

(Honey also inspired the common phrase *sweetness and light*. Jonathan Swift coined this mellifluous expression when he wrote that bees produce honey and wax, "thus furnishing mankind with the two noblest things, which are sweetness and light.")

mess When those in medieval England spoke of a *mess*, they meant a "course of a meal." This type of *mess* (as well as the French *mets*, "food") is the etymological offspring of the Late Latin word *missus*, which literally describes something "sent forth." Thus, the English *mess* shares a common linguistic ancestor with such "sending" words as *transmit, mission,* and *message*.

Like many other food words, *mess* was eventually also put to a more negative use, in this case denoting a "jumbled, confused situation" or "cluttered, dirty condition." By 1854, Miss Anne E.

Baker defined *mess* in her *Glossary of Northampton-shire Words and Phrases* as "a hodge-podge, or dirty, disagreeable mixture. Any culinary preparation that is unpalatable would be called 'a nasty mess.' " (Another food term of sorts denoting a "mess" or "jumble of wildly different items" is *dog's breakfast*. The origin of this expression will be readily apparent to anyone who's ever taken a pup on a morning stroll. It was used this way, for example, by a British newspaper writer in 1959: "He can't make head or tail of it. . . . It's a complete dog's breakfast.")

moxie In the late 1800s, "Moxie Nerve Food" was a tart, bracing beverage sold throughout northern New England. Dr. Augustine Thompson marketed his elixir as a remedy for "paralysis, softening of the brain, and mental imbecility" and tirelessly promoted it with the perkily prescriptive slogan "What this country needs is plenty of Moxie!" The saying caught on, and *moxie* soon meant "courage," "shrewdness," and "energetic initiative."

Dr. Thompson claimed he had named the drink after a West Point classmate named Lieutenant Moxie, who allegedly had discovered its secret ingredients while traveling in a remote area of South America. However, this story is suspect for several reasons, such as the fact that Dr. Thompson never attended West Point. Then again, maybe the physician was just showing a little moxie himself.

mundungus Here's a word that's definitely worth reviving. Surprisingly, however, misocapnists—that is, people who loathe smoke from cigarettes, cigars, or pipes—still haven't seized upon this term for "stinky tobacco." *Mundungus* itself has an even more odoriferous background: the word is a humorous adaptation of the Spanish *mondongo,* a word for "tripe," the stomach lining of various animals that shows up in dishes of various cuisines.

Sir Walter Scott used the redolent word *mundungus* in 1824, describing a character's "jet black cutty pipe, from which she soon sent . . . clouds of vile *mundungus* vapour." Fifteen years later an impassioned pamphleteer shuddered at the memory of someone who was, in his words, "offending the nostrils of all misocapnists with the fumes of his *mundungus.*"

mutt Because sheep are traditionally assumed to be stupid, the word *muttonhead* came to be applied to any person considered dull-witted or ignorant. At the turn of this century, speakers of English clipped *muttonhead* to *mutt* and began to use this word in reference to people rather than animals. Then in 1904, the *Oxford English Dictionary* explains, a writer contemptuously applied the word *mutt* to a horse. Two years later, another used it to refer to a dog, exclaiming, "A fellow can't leave nothin' on his bed without that mutt chawin' it up!" Over time, this word inspired by sheep meat came to specify a *mongrel,* or mixed-breed pup, *mongrel* itself being a close linguistic relative of such "mixing" words as *mingle* and *among.*

Speaking of mutton, *to give someone the cold shoulder* may refer not to turning one's back but to the old practice of serving unwelcome company a cold shoulder of mutton, as opposed to a warm, lovingly prepared meal. Scholars are divided on the authenticity of this story, but if such chilly hospitality is indeed the source of this expression, a cold shoulder of mutton might be considered what the French call a *chasse-cousin.* This term applies to anything served in a similarly grudging fashion — a meager dinner or bad wine, for example — in a calculated effort to "chase away cousins" and other unwelcome guests.

Incidentally, a boorish guest who overstays his welcome may turn his reluctant host into what the French call a *mouton enragé,* or "angry sheep," a relative of *mutt* and *mutton.* This expression has been borrowed whole into English, where *mouton enragé* is a jocular metaphor for "a normally calm person who suddenly becomes enraged or violent."

nucleus The Latin word *nuculus,* or "little nut," lies at the heart of this word for the "kernel" or "central portion around which other parts are arranged," such as the heaviest part of an atom, the *nucleus.* The Latin word *nux,* or "nut," is also tucked inside *nougat,* a nut-filled confection of sugar or honey paste, and *noisette,* a small, round piece of meat.

pabulum, pablum The word *pabulum* can mean both "nourishing food" and "insipid, nonnourishing intellectual fare." That's because in ancient Rome, *pabulum* simply meant "food," "nourishment," or "fodder," and for years this word carried the same meaning in English. In the early 1930s, however, Mead Johnson & Company of Evansville, Indiana, obtained a patent for a breakfast cereal that featured a mixture of wheat meal to which was added some "wheat embryo, dried yeast, powdered dehydrated alfalfa leaf and powdered beef bone prepared for human use." Sounds nutritious, and it is—which is why they marketed it under a trademark name formed from the Latin word for nourishing fare, *pabulum.* As time went on, however, *Pablum* baby cereal became so popular that people began associating the name with anything that was similarly bland and mushy, particularly writing that is trite, dull, or overly simplistic.

paste Though this word now applies to everything from dentifrice to a point-and-click command on a computer screen, its humble origins lie in the ancient Greek word for "barley porridge," *pastos,* from the Greek *passein,* "to sprinkle." The English adopted the Greek word's Old French descendant, *paste,* in the fourteenth century and ap-

177

plied it to moist, kneaded flour. It would be another century and a half before *paste* was also applied, as it were, to "glue." To the same doughy etymological family belongs the name of that English meat pie known as a *pasty,* as well as the words *pastry, pasta,* and *pâté.*

pearl The faint linguistic outline of a ham may be visible inside this word for the lustrous loot snatched from mollusks. That's the contention of many etymologists, who note that such ancient Roman writers as Pliny applied the name *perna,* or "ham," to a certain sea mussel that has a ham-shaped shell. These scholars suspect that a diminutive form, *pernula,* eventually evolved into our word *pearl.* Another possible explanation suggests that *pearl* comes from an entirely different food word: *pirula,* a diminutive of the Latin *pirum,* "pear," because imperfect pearls are often pear-shaped.

pemmican From the Cree Indians, English settlers borrowed a recipe for dried, pounded meat mixed with melted fat, then pressed into hard cakes. *Pemmican* was long a food of choice for those in need of a nourishing high-calorie but compact comestible that would keep for a long time, and it is still used by Arctic travelers. By extension, this word also means "densely written prose" or anything similarly condensed. In 1892, one writer rightly noted that "The modern man is but rarely inclined to read his history in many volumes. He much prefers it pemmicanized." A few years later, another presciently observed, "What one may call the era of the Pemmicanisation of life is rapidly approaching."

placenta Early anatomists called this flat, circular organ the *placenta uterina,* or "uterine cake," from the Latin *placenta,* meaning "flat cake." Attached to the fetus via the umbilical cord, it has a name that belongs to a rather large etymological family of "flat" words, including *plank,* which arrived in English from Latin via French. From the Germanic languages, English inherited several "flat" linguistic cousins of *plank* and *placenta,* including *flake* and *fluke* (a "flatfish"), as well as the flat walkway material called *flagstone* and the creamy, flat dessert *flan.* Another food word that belongs in this "flat" family is the German word *Fladen,* which can mean either a "flat cake," or, less appetizingly, a "cowpat."[4]

potpourri The fragrant mixture of dried flowers and spices popularly called *potpourri* gets its name from the surprisingly unsavory French term *pot pourri,* literally "rotten pot." In fact, *potpourri* is a close etymological relative of such English words

---

[4] From an unrelated Sanskrit family of "flat" words comes the Sanskrit word for "flat," *carpata,* which gave rise, as it were, to the name of the flat Indian bread called a *chapati.*

as *putrid, putrify,* and *pus.* (Another relative is the French name for the whippoorwill, *bois-pourri,* or "rotten wood," from the belief that this bird makes its home inside rotting logs.)

Potpourri is a translation of the Spanish *olla podrida,* a term originally applied to a spicy boiled stew also called an *olio.* Both Spanish terms now reside in English as well. One seventeenth-century writer observed that the dish called an *olio* "is a very great one, contayning in it diuers things, as Mutton, Beefe, Hens, Capons, Sawsages, Piggs feete, Garlick, Onions, &c. It is called Podrida, because it is sod leisurely, til it be rotten (as we say) and ready to fall in peeces. . . . In English it may well beare the name of Hodge-podge."

(These aren't the only dishes with seemingly self-deprecating names. A popular puff pastry in Hawaii, for example, is the *malasado,* which originated among Portuguese immigrants. It's made by tossing scraps of sweet bread dough into hot fat, creating a bread whose name literally means "badly baked.")

Like *hodgepodge, salmagundi, farrago,* and *gallimaufry,* the word *potpourri* now applies to nonculinary mixtures as well. So does *olla podrida,* as in the case of a nineteenth-century letter writer's reference to "That olla-podrida of a brain of mine."

potshot As early as the 1850s, a *potshot* was an easy shot that hunters took at close range, solely for the purpose of filling the cooking pot for that evening. Later it came to extend in a metaphorical sense to any shoot-from-the-hip or below-the-belt attack on the defenseless. A *potboiler*, on the other hand, is a literary work written solely for money — that is, in order to continue to stock one's cooking pot and keep it boiling.[5]

The phrase *go to pot*, however, preserves the faint image of someone cutting up meat to go into a boiling pot. In sixteenth- and seventeenth-century manuscripts, this expression often appeared as *to go to the pot*. Nowadays *to go to pot* is to be ruined or destroyed — in other words, to go to pieces.

Of course, no discussion of *pot* would be complete without a mention of the kind that's smoked. *Pot* used as slang for "marijuana" may come from the Mexican Spanish *potiguaya*, short for *potación de guaya*, or "drink of grief" — a name that refers to the time-honored practice of soaking marijuana buds in wine or brandy for a little added grief-chasing effect.

pukka Pronounced "PUCK-ah," this word means "sure, certain, reliable" or "factually correct." *Pukka* entered English during the seventeenth century

---

[5] A similar image appears in the story about how a well-known Michigan city got its name: inspired by the presence of gas bubbles at one turbulent point in a nearby river, settlers there adapted a Native American expression thought to mean "boiling pot" and proceeded to call both the river and the city *Kalamazoo*.

as an adaptation of the Hindi *pakkā,* meaning "cooked" or "ripe," and shares a common linguistic ancestor with several culinary words, including *cook, kitchen, cuisine,* the "twice-cooked" food *biscuit,* and the "re-cooked" cheese *ricotta.* These words are also kin to *precocious,* from the Latin *prae-,* or "pre-" and *coquere,* "to cook" or "to ripen." In its earliest sense, the English word *precocious* applied to a plant or flower that bloomed early or bore fruit before others did and only later referred in a more abstract sense to children who develop faster than their peers. A close relative of *precocious,* by the way, is the name of that "early-ripening" fruit, the *apricot.*

razz According to an 1890 dictionary of slang, the verb *razz* means "to tease" and is a shortening of *raspberry,* that contemptuous wet sputter made by fluttering one's tongue through protruded lips to produce "a peculiarly squashy noise that is extremely irritating." Another turn-of-the-century source likens this sound to "the rending of glazed calico."

But how exactly did this wet sputter, also known as a *Bronx cheer,* come to be associated with a little red berry in the first place? The explanation lies in the Cockney tradition of rhyming slang, a playful invented language allowing those in the know to converse privately even when others are around—as when, for example, Cockney parents use the code phrases *Gawd forbids* to mean "kids," *bread and honey* to mean "money," and *I should cocoa* for "I should say so." The noisy *raspberry* gets its name from the fact that in Cockney rhyming slang, the expression *raspberry tart* is a euphemism for "fart."

rhubarb This ruddy vegetable's name is also used as a synonym for "simulated chatter or hubbub in movies or plays." The reason lies in the long-standing theatrical tradition of having actors in crowd scenes repeat the word *rhubarb*, as well as other expressions, such as "peas and carrots" and "my fiddle, my fiddle," in order to appear as if they're really saying something. This noisy sense of *rhubarb* has contributed to the word's use as a synonym for a "quarrel, heated discussion, or fight." This food's name, in any case; is thought by many scholars to have arisen from the ancient Greeks' name for the Volga River, *Rha*, on the shores of which they first found this plant.

salary In ancient, prerefrigerated times, salt was so valued as a preservative that Roman soldiers received a regular allowance to buy it. The Latin name for this allowance for salt, or *sāl*, was known as the *salārium*. Later this term came to be applied more generally to a soldier's pay, and eventually it gave rise to the English word *salary*.

A linguistic cousin of the English *salt*, the Latin *sal* also produced the flavorful words *salsa* and *sauce*. An alcohol drinker who has hit the sauce too much is said to be *soused*, which, as it happens, is another "salt" word. *To souse* originally meant "to pickle meat by steeping it in a briny solution." (One preacher used this notion to colorful, if questionable, effect in an early-eighteenth-century sermon, imploring his God to "Sowse us therefore in the Powdering-Tub of thy Mercy, that we may be Tripes fit for the Heavenly Table.")

Another member of this word family is the name of the spicy meat *sausage*, a particularly salty variety of which is the etymologically related *salami*. Two other food names that share this salty linguistic pedigree: the English *salad*, from the Latin *herba salāta*, or "salted herbs," so called because such greens were usually seasoned with dressings containing lots of salt, and the Greek salad of fish roe, olive oil, lemon juice, and moist bread crumbs or mashed potatoes, *taramasalata* — from *tarama*, a Turkish word for "roe."

The English *salad*, interestingly, is also part of at least two useful expressions. One is *salad days*, referring to a time of youthful inexperience. This term apparently was coined by Shakespeare, whose Cleopatra characterizes her long-ago romance with Julius Caesar as one occurring in "my salad days, when I was green in judgment, cold in blood." *Salad* also has the distinction of being part of a bona fide psychiatric term. According to *Webster's Third New International Dictionary*, psychiatrists sometimes use the vivid expression *word salad* to denote "the extreme incoherence of schiz-ophrenics."

salver At mealtime in medieval royal households, servants carried drinks to the diners on trays called *salvers*. This name arose from the act of tasting royal food and drink to check for spoilage or poisoning, a preprandial ritual that the Spaniards called a *salva*, from *salvar*, "to save," a relative of *salvation*, *safe*, and *salvage*. Today the English word *salver* applies to any type of tray, especially those used to present food.

Other words that share a common ancestor with *salver* include *salubrious* and *sage*, as in the herb. Originally used more in medicine than in cooking, this aromatic plant was known to the Romans as *salvia*, from the Latin *salvus*, "healthy." *Salvia* moved into Old French as *sauge*, a name borrowed into Middle English and eventually altered to the familiar name for this herb. (The other kind of *sage*, as in a wise person, comes from the Latin *sapere*, "to know," a verb whose meaning evolved from its earlier sense, "to taste." From *sapere* also come such "tasting" words as *savor* and such "knowing" words as *savvy*, *savant*, *savoir-faire*, and the *sapiens* in the name of that allegedly wise species, *Homo sapiens*.)

satire The drama festivals of ancient Rome often featured medleys of satirical verse that lampooned contemporary follies or vices. This mixture of various kinds of poetry was affectionately known as a *lanx satura,* or "full dish," alluding to the tradition of piling a variety of foods onto a plate and then sacrificing it to the gods. The name eventually evolved into the English *satire,* a word probably reinforced by the fact that many ancient plays featured running commentary from a chorus of those lusty beings called *satyrs* or, in Greek, *satyroi.* Today a theatrical production that is *satirical* holds someone or something up to ridicule, while *satyrical* specifically indicates an ancient Greek play featuring those hoofed creatures.

Incidentally, the *lanx,* or "dish," in the expression *lanx satura* was also a word for either of the two dishes attached to the type of scale used for weighing. This dish is still visible in the English word *balance,* which comes from the Latin *bilanx,* literally "two-dish." In addition, the *satura* in *lanx satura* is related to several English words concerning fullness, including *satisfy, saturate, insatiable,* and even the word *sad,* which in its earliest sense meant "having had one's fill" of something. In fact, like the word *full, sad*'s ancestor in Old English was commonly used with *of,* so that, in 1200, a penitent writer would speak of being "sad of mine sinnes." *Sad* continued a fascinating evolution over the centuries: in the early 1300s, the word *sad* meant "steadfast, firm, constant." A hundred years later it meant "trustworthy" or "valiant," so that one early-fifteenth-century writer could describe something that "maketh a man more strong and more *saᗡ* [against] his Enemyes." Around the same time, *saᗡ* could be used to mean "intelligent" ("full of learning," in other words) and soon also acquired the meaning that we associate with it today—describing someone who is "full" of the world and burdened with its cares.

The connection between *saᗡ* and "fullness" or "heaviness" reappeared in seventeenth- and eighteenth-century cookbooks, in which it described bread that has not risen properly and therefore feels heavy. One cookbook writer tried to steer readers away from a particular cooking mistake, warning, "It makes the crust sad, and is a great hazard of the pie running." Which, come to think of it, would make for a very full dish indeed.

ᗡeerᘛucker One of the most delicious words in the English language, *ᗡeerᘛucker* is adapted from the Hindi word *ᘛīrᘛakar*, which literally means "milk and sugar" and refers to the alternating crinkles and stripes on seersucker fabric. The Hindi word was borrowed from Persian, which in turn derived the *-ᘛucker* part from the Sanskrit *ᘛarkarā*, which originally meant "gravel" or "grit" and later, "sugar." These words belong to a sweet family that includes *ᘛaccharine*, as well as the English *ᘛugar* and its cognates in several languages, including the Spanish *azúcar*, French *ᘛucre*, Italian *zucchero*, and German *Zucker*.

(The Sanskrit word *śarkarā,* meaning "sugar" or "gravel," also shares a common ancestor with the Greek word for "pebble," *krokē*—a word preserved, oddly enough, in our own word *crocodile.* But what is the etymological connection between crocodiles and pebbles? According to the ancient historian Herodotus, when early Greeks traveling in Egypt encountered a small and unfamiliar type of lizard, they dubbed it a *krokodilos,* a combination of the words *krokē,* "pebble," and *drilos,* which in ancient Greek meant either "circumcised man" or "worm." The historian, whose accounts were often unreliable but always entertaining, speculated that Greek men traveling abroad had jokingly christened the reptile *krokodilos* because they were struck by the resemblance between the basking lizards and their own "worm of the stones," so to speak. Thus one ancient linguistic ancestor may have spawned such far-flung and picturesque progeny as *sugar, crocodiles,* and *seersucker.*)

shambles Although today the word *shambles* can apply to anything from a messy room to a disintegrating political career, it derives from the Middle English word *shamel,* which meant "a portable stall in a marketplace for the butchering and sale of meat." For some three hundred years after that, the word *shambles* specifically meant "slaughterhouse."

Shambles is one of the many English words now drained of their earlier, more vivid, and often unsavory meanings. Another chilling example: *dreary*. Although today it describes anything that's merely "dismal," "boring," or "repulsively dull or uninteresting," its Old English predecessor, *drēorig*, meant "bloody," or "gory." When it appears in the epic poem *Beowulf*, for example, the adjective *drēorig* applies to a pool of water reddened by the blood of a decapitated warrior.

sitophobia Contrary to appearances, someone who is sitophobic isn't destined to stand up all of his or her life for fear of sitting down. This little-used but still quite relevant word comes from the Greek *phobos*, "fear," and *sītos*, "food," and means a "morbid fear of food."

Sit Greek *sītos* down beside the Greek prefix *para-*, meaning "alongside" (as in *parallel*, literally "beside each other," and *paranoid*, "beside the mind" or, in other words, "distracted") and the result is *parasite*, someone or something that "feeds alongside its host." In ancient Greece, a *parasitos* was someone who belonged to a class of priests' assistants, whose duty it was to set up the elaborate banquets that usually followed a sacrifice to the gods. These underlings traditionally were rewarded with an invitation to dine at the priests' table, and for that reason they were known as *parasitoi*, or "parasites"—literally, "the ones dining alongside." As an eighteenth-century English writer would later explain, in antiquity the term *parasite* had specified "the Priest's Guest, whom he invited to eat part of the Sacrifice: whence the word is taken for a smell-feast."

(*Smell-feast?* The *Oxford English Dictionary* defines it as "One who scents out where feasting is to be had; one who comes uninvited to share in a feast; a parasite, a greedy sponger." The term *smell-feast* was quite popular during the latter half of the sixteenth century and throughout the seventeenth; considering its sneering efficiency and practical applicability, one wonders why it ever dropped out of favor.)

The Greek word *parasitos*, at any rate, also came to mean anyone who was metaphorically "dining at the table of another." An adaptation of its Latinized form, *parasitus*, appeared in English in the sixteenth century, so that by 1607 Shakespeare's Timon of Athens could rage, "You knot of Mouth-Friends: . . . Most smiling, smooth, detested Parasites." (Incidentally, in contrast to a parasite, which feeds at the expense of its hosts, a *commensal* is an animal or plant that attaches to another and shares its food, as in the case of certain species of sea anemones that attach to crabs. This word also has been applied to a person who shares food equally with another—a "messmate" or "companion," in other words. *Commensal* comes from the Latin *com-*, "together with," and *mensa*, "table," *mensa* also appearing in the modern English name of an organization intended as a kind of round-table for those with above-average IQs, *Mensa*.)

slush fund Although today the term *slush fund* often conjures up images of money secretly stashed away for corrupt politicians, this expression originated in the sailors' word *slush*, which meant the "excess fat or grease left over after boiling meat" aboard ship. As W. McNally explained in an 1839 work, *Evils & Abuses in Naval & Merchant Service*, "The sailors in the navy are allowed salt beef. . . . From this provision, when cooked . . . nearly all the fat boils off; this is carefully skimmed . . . and put into empty beef or pork barrels, and sold, and the money so received is called the *slush fund*." By selling their slush to soap and candle makers, the sailors obtained discretionary funds for less-than-discreet entertainments onshore.

snoop These days the word *snoop* is most often used in connection with prying photographers or reporters who dig up dish on someone by stealthy means. Originally, however, *snoop* referred to obtaining a very different type of dish. The word *snoop* is an adaptation of the Dutch *snoepen*, meaning "to eat sweets on the sly" or, as the *Oxford English Dictionary* describes it, "to appropriate and consume dainties in a clandestine manner." Indeed, in the mid–nineteenth century Americans still used *snoop* in both senses—so that it was possible for a *snoop* to *snoop* while *snooping* on someone who was *snooping*.

spam As the so-called information superhighway continues to expand, more and more computer users run the risk of being spammed. But they won't be ducking tins of *Spam,* whose name is a condensed form of that product's contents, "spiced ham." In recent years, computer hackers have converted this noun into a verb, using it to mean "to crash a computer program by entering an excessive amount of data." The verb *to spam* later expanded to mean "to flood an on-line newsgroup with irrelevant or inappropriate messages," the most famous being one in which some lawyers tried to solicit business on line by flooding the Internet with ads for their firm. Other spammings include the electronic equivalent of a chain letter and endless postings that proclaim the imminent end of the world.

But how did the odoriferous pink cube of compressed meat come to mean "to overwhelm with information"? The answer, on-line experts say, arises from the immortal *Monty Python* sketch in which a restaurant customer asks what's on the menu and the waiter replies, "Well, there's egg and bacon; egg, sausage, and bacon; egg, bacon, and Spam; egg, bacon, sausage, and Spam; Spam, bacon, sausage, and Spam; Spam, egg, Spam, Spam, bacon, and Spam; Spam, Spam, Spam, egg, and Spam; Spam, Spam, Spam, Spam, Spam, Spam, baked beans, Spam, Spam, Spam, and Spam; or lobster thermidor aux crevettes with a mornay sauce garnished with truffle pâté, brandy, and a fried egg on top of Spam." As anyone who's ever received unsolicited E-mail can attest, the annoying experience of being *spammed* electronically is enough to leave you feeling like the besieged listener who just lost his appetite.

sycophant This word for a "servile flatterer" or "parasite" comes from the Greek word *sukophantes*, literally "the one showing a fig," although it's never been clear just what sort of fig-showing this expression implies. Plutarch suggested that the word derives from the fact that it was once illegal to export figs from Attica without paying a tax, so that anyone who finked on the fig shippers was said to be a *sucophantes*—that is, "someone who shows the fig" to government officials.

However, a double entendre may be at work here because the Greek word for "fig," *sukon*, also meant "female genitalia," an allusion to the suggestive appearance of a split, ripened fig. Similarly, in Italian, where the word for "fig" is *fico* (a relative of the English *fig* and *ficus*), a slight alteration produced *fica*, a word denoting both a vulgar sexual reference to a woman and an obscene gesture suggesting the same, made by thrusting the thumb either between two fingers or into the mouth. A thief named Vanni Fucci put this gesture of contempt to memorable use in Dante's *Inferno* when, not at all happy about having gone to hell, "the thief — to his disgrace — raised his hands with both fists making figs, and cried, 'Here, God! I throw them in your face!'" This scornful gesture also figures in Shakespeare's *Henry V,* where characters call it either *figo* or *the fig of Spain.*)

Back to *sukophantes:* over time, this Greek word came to denote not only a "tattler" but a "blackmailer," "professional swindler," "con artist," and "ingratiating flatterer," and when a version of its Latin descendant was adopted into English as *sycophant,* it carried all of those meanings as well.

Incidentally, the *sukon,* or "fig," inside *sycophant* also appears in the name of the fig-bearing *sycamore tree.* This tree, mentioned in ancient scripture, is a different species from the one that goes by the same name in North America, which therefore sometimes has the qualifiers *bastard, false,* or *vulgar* in its name before the word *sycamore.* The *-phant* in *sycophant,* by the way, derives from the Greek verb *phainein,* meaning "to show," which also gave us *fantasy* and *phenomenon,* as well as the theological word *theophany,* which literally means "appearance of a god," the linguistic ghost of which appears in the feminine name that means the same thing, *Tiffany.*)

symposium Although nowadays we think of a *symposium* as a formal meeting or conference, such a gathering in ancient times involved lots of carousing and lampooning, because the Romans used the word *symposium* specifically to mean "a drinking party." A derivative of the Greek *sumposion*, literally a "drinking-with," the word *symposium* is a linguistic relative of such terms as *potable* and *potion*.

tarsal In ancient Greek, the word *tarsos* means "a wicker mat for drying cheese," a word fashioned from a much earlier ancient term meaning "to dry up." *Tarsos*, in turn, evolved in sense so that it came to denote several kinds of similarly flat objects, including the sole of the foot. The etymological outlines of this word are visible in the medical *tarsals*, any of several small foot bones, and in the name of their anatomical neighbors, the *metatarsals*.

treacle This word for "cloying words or sentiment" is a borrowing of the commonly used British word for what Americans call *molasses*. The linguistic history of the word *treacle* itself goes all the way back to the Greek word for "wild animal," *thēr*, a relative of *feral, fierce*, and *ferocious*. In ancient Greece, a *thēriakē* was an antidote against the poisonous bite of a wild animal. By Chaucer's time, the English descendant of this word, *triacle*, denoted a type of medicinal antidote purported to cure not only venomous bites but other ailments as well.[6] Not long afterward, charlatans began making these compounds more palatable by adding molasses and other ingredients, and by the late seventeenth century, the meaning of the word *treacle* had shifted to the sweetening agent itself.[7] Speaking of antidotes to poison, the name of the long root vegetable *scorzonera* refers to its alleged antivenom qualities. Its name derives from the Italian *scorzone,* or "poisonous snake," most likely an allusion to its use as an antidote to snakebites.

tsimmes Originally, this Yiddish word of uncertain origin meant a "stew" or "casserole" usually containing sweetened vegetables and fruit. But its jumble of ingredients proved to be an irresistible

---

[6] In fact, when some early English translators of the Bible were casting about for a better way to translate the famous passage in Jeremiah 8:22 ("Is there no balm in Gilead; is there no physician there?"), they used the word *treacle* instead of *balm.* As a result, such pre–King James versions of the Bible sometimes go by the name *Treacle Bibles.*

[7] As every Scrabble player should know, another colorful "antidote" word is *bezoar.* Deriving from Persian for "poison protector," the word *bezoar* is defined in *The American Heritage Dictionary* as "A hard indigestible mass of material, such as hair, vegetable fibers, or fruits, found in the stomachs or intestines of animals, especially ruminants, and human beings." In the past, the dictionary goes on to explain, a *bezoar* was "considered to be an antidote to poisons and to possess magic properties."

metaphor for any confused situation or fuss, as in "Why are you making such a *tsimmes* over everything?"

uvula The little teardrop-shaped part of the soft palate hanging down at the back of the throat takes its name from the Latin *ūvula,* which means "little grape" and is the diminutive of the Latin *ūva,* or grape, which is also part of *uvate,* a not-very-common name for "grape jam." In addition, this fruit's name was plucked from Latin and altered into the anatomical name for that rounded inner layer of an eyeball, the *uvea.*[8]

zest The roots of this word for "gusto" or "keen enjoyment" go back as far as the French word *zeste,* meaning either the "peel of an orange or lemon" or the "thick skin quartering the kernel of a walnut." There, however, the etymological trail turns cold. The first use of the word *zest* was recorded in 1674, referring to an orange peel squeezed into wine for a little extra zing. Just over a century later, it came to connote a more abstract sense of "passionate enjoyment" or "relish."

---

[8] The grape-shaped uvula has inspired no end of picturesque names in other languages. In Danish, a uvula is a *drøpel*—a "little drop." To Spanish speakers it's a *campanilla,* or "little bell," while Germans call it a *Zäpfchen,* or "little peg." In Russian, a uvula is a *jazychok,* or "little tongue," and in Swedish, it's a *tungspene,* or "tongue teat."

zydeco That foot-stomping, washboard-scraping, accordion-squeezing, fiddle-sawing southern Louisiana music known as *zydeco* may owe its name to beans—or at least to some has-been beans. Many linguists believe that *zydeco* stems from the Creole pronunciation of *les haricots*, or, in French, "beans"—an expression that appears in the oft-repeated refrain of one of the earliest and most popular zydeco songs, "*Les haricots sont pas salé*," literally, "The beans aren't salty."

ACKNOWLEDGMENTS

$\mathcal{L}$ike the proverbial stone soup, this language lovers' feast has been enriched by the contributions of many individuals. Translator Clara Cerón generously shared both her insistent expertise and consistent good humor. The knowledgeable denizens of the CompuServe Information Service provided a wealth of information, and I'm particularly grateful to those who put up with my questions on the Cooks Forum, Foreign Language Education Forum, Italian Forum, Issues Forum, Pacific Forum, Japan Forum, and Netherlands Forum. Melody Mazuk somehow managed to gather more German cookie names than I dreamed could exist.

Others who provided essential ingredients and inspiration include Henlee Barnette, Wayne Barnette, Diether Betche, Polly C. Blakemore, Polly W. Blakemore, Harry Blumenthal, Paolo Bottoni, Tilmar Brandl, Heine Brothers, Ulisses W. Carvalho, Raoul Clem, Lisa de Araujo, Hans Eberstark, Maureen Fant, Elaine Felhandler, Russell Galen, Lon Hall, Lucas J. Hogan, Barbara Joost, Hansje Kalff, Eiko Kanamaru, Michael Keizer, Susan Krauss of Krauss Research in Oakland, Lilian Lim, Margarita Lliteras, Susanna Malm, John McGhee, Molly McGinnis, Corien Meijvogel, Jackie Murgida, W. M. O'Riley, Mary O'Shaughnessy, Monique Popescu, Erroll Rhodes,

Evi Silvia, Virginia Sinai, Oma Steeneken, Sue Steeneken, Annie Veranda, T. Alvin Veranda, Martin Voglmaier, Carla Wallace, K. J. Wibbeke, Lynn Winter, and Christa Zorn.

I'm grateful as always to my editor, Ruth Fecych, for her enthusiasm, support, and guidance, and to agent Gail E. Ross for introducing us. I'm hugely indebted to Lynn Anderson for her deft and keen-eyed copyediting.

Special thanks to word lover and massage therapist extraordinaire Sally Marcum, whose ministrations made all the difference. Thanks also to Louisville *Courier-Journal* restaurant critic Susan Reigler, who cheerfully delivered armfuls of food books to my door and never once laughed at my writing clothes. I'm grateful as well for the usual writerly support and sustenance from Pamela Robin Brandt, Robin Garr, Judith Newman, Kay Turner, and Lindsy Van Gelder.

To the woman who set an example as a lifelong learner and lovingly advised me to "just let you be you": Thanks, Mom.

Finally, thanks as always to my partner in life and love, Louisville artist Debra Clem.

Louisville, Kentucky
April 1997

INDEX

Index

0-595-34503-4

Printed in the United States
29922LVS00001B/197